University Education in India

Issues, Implications & Alternatives

Ishwar Dayal

Former Director,

Indian Institute of Management

Lucknow

Ane Books Pvt. Ltd.

New Delhi ♦ Chennai

University Education in India
Issues, Implications & Alternatives

Ishwar Dayal

Price : Rs.795/-
Pages : xii+146=158 (HB)
Size : 5.50" x 8.50"
Paper Quality (GSM) : 80

Published by

Ane Books Pvt. Ltd.
4821, Parwana Bhawan, 1st Floor, 24 Ansari Road, Darya Ganj,
New Delhi - 110 002, Tel.: +91(011) 23276843-44, Fax: +91(011) 23276863
e-mail: kapoor@anebooks.com, Website: www.anebooks.com

Branch

- Avantika Niwas, 1st Floor, 19 Doraiswamy Road, T. Nagar,
  Chennai - 600 017, Tel.: +91(044) 28141554, 28141209
  e-mail: anebookschennai@gmail.com, rathinam@anebooks.com

ISBN : 978-81-8052-272-7

Printed at : R.K. Offset Process, New Delhi.

Preface

Education in society has as important a function as business, public services, political institutions and other such activity centres. Each has a recognisable and contributory function for society to remain balanced and dynamic. In broad terms, the function of education is to provide a knowledge-base, contribute to the social and technical advancement, value-orientation, understanding the processes of change at societal and institutional level, etc. The business and other economic systems have to generate wealth by undertaking activities in industrial production, trade and commerce, etc. Public services are created to provide multiple services to people. The functions of all these are interlinked and ultimately contribute to the well-being of the society and quality of life for the citizen. This is a highly simplified formulation of a complex network of functions and tasks but, in essence, represents a basic relationship and an overview of a dynamic society.

This book concerns the inter-relationship of education and society; in particular, university level education. This is based on my active involvement of around 50 years with the university system. However, the considerations in my elaboration apply equally to other levels of educational system.

Some basic questions that need serious examination are :

1. Why is it that a university system, in the sixty years after India's independence, has generated very limited knowledge-base as compared to similar educational bodies in the West in spite of comparable intellectual capital in both situations?
2. Why is it that industry as well as social and professional institutions continue to look to the West for knowledge in many critical areas of societal and technological development?
3. What is the role that educational system performs in a society? Is this role different in some significant ways in a developing society such as India, or the same as in the West? What is the nature of interdependence between the educational system and the society in which it operates?

A discussion on these questions is important to reflect on what should be the requirement of the university system in our country, and its role in respect to other activity centres and the society. These concerns are relevant because in the emerging socio-cultural and economic environment continuing knowledge-base of technological advancement, value-orientation, innovation, and professional competence would determine the country's standing in the world society.

After World War II, world leaders like Roosevelt, Nehru, General D'Gaul and others had taken steps to develop institutions to research on processes of cooperation, resolving conflict in constructive ways, and understanding differences among nations and people. Many educational and research institutions were created or supported by many countries to work on these areas and on many other social and societal issues. Besides universities and special institutions, world bodies such as the United Nations and its related bodies in professional and specialised areas were created. All these have provided valuable understanding in social, technical, and human sciences. Notwithstanding the knowledge available in these and related areas, the countries individually and collectively have at best been able to contain conflict but not avoid it. However, there is little evidence that many of the findings of social science research are applied in government systems, social, and business organisations and in academic institutions. In the main the knowledge-base has remained locked up in-between the covers of books.

This book concerns university and technical education in general with emphasis on management education. The reason for this choice of management education is that of my close association as a teacher, director, consultant, adviser and member of several committees in management education and I could look at it from within and from outside the system. However, my discussion with other professional educational programmes, except medical, suggests that they share similar concerns as brought out in respect to management education.

For my incentive to write this book, I am obliged to Mr. Satya Narayanan, Chairman of Career Launcher, for his enthusiastic references to university education, and extremely positive outlook in whatever he does. I began to seriously review my experiences and readings of the university system and exchanged ideas with several persons who have interest in the subject. The present volume is an outcome of these efforts. I have read some papers on management education and published some in journals. These have been re-written for this volume but include several ideas from these papers.

There is a tendency in most developing countries, including India, to have the practices prevailing in the West as a reference point under the belief that they offer a model. I contend that reference point for developing a system should be the society, not the West, because education has a significant role in the process of advancement of knowledge-base in society. This in fact is the reference point of this book. There is much to learn from the experience and the processes prevailing in the West but these have to be adapted to the local situation.

I am grateful to my colleagues at the Indus World School of Business, specially to Mr. Somonnoy Ghosh, for the exchange of ideas, and Mr. Daljeet Charkhandi for patiently typing many revisions of the chapters in this book. Somonnoy was also kind enough to write chapter 2 on thoughts through age on higher education.

The strength of our educational system in ancient period was discourse and dialectic approaches to learning. I hope we are able to examine the suggestions in this book in the spirit of the old. This is my hope.

Mr. Sunil Saxena, Chairman of Ane Books Pvt. Ltd. and his colleagues have been most helpful in bringing the book out. My thanks to them.

New Delhi **Ishwar Dayal**

Contents

1

A Concept of a University

After the World War II, President Roosevelt in mid 1940s had declared that the second half of the century will be different from the first half. A large number of institutions were set up to generate knowledge in physical and social sciences that could contribute to understanding of and develop cooperation among people and among nations, and contribute to enhance the quality of life. It was assumed that if knowledge is available it would be used for the well-being of the people, and such institutions would highlight processes to strengthen peace and harmony among people and among nations. A great deal of knowledge is indeed created in social and physical science, and development of technology, but there is little evidence that this is used especially in the management of institutions, and conduct of societal, national and international issues.

It is indeed rare to see that the knowledge generated in social sciences forms a basis for conducting affairs of institutions or in policy-making. The generation of knowledge and then applying it appear to be two different processes. In many ways society has used the findings of physical sciences and technology, and relatively less the knowledge obtained in social sciences, to develop institutions and relationships. Even teaching universities and institutions rarely use findings in behavioural and organisational research for building institutions. In this book, I have attempted to use research findings in developing the concept of a university and methodologies effective for educational inputs. I have employed the available findings of social sciences in developing a conceptual framework.

Educational institutions should serve as pivotal institutions to bring about social consciousness in society, and for the development of viable and purposeful institutions. If an educational system tends to become ineffective, or is frozen in the past, either foreign prescriptions are imposed upon the system or it becomes static. In the either scenario academic community and those who need knowledge inputs for their growth begin to ignore the educational system, and look elsewhere for new and relevant inputs. The educational system in India seems to be approaching this stage. The value system, the dynamism in society in a large measure, is linked to the dynamism and character of the education in the country. Education should not be confused with literacy, however important this might be. Being closely associated with professional education for about fifty years, I would look critically at the system of technical education at the university level, also contending that in-depth examination of education in other areas is just as important. I believe that what is highlighted for professional education applies in essence to the system as a whole. If we were to view the inclusive role of education in society and for institutional development, we require a comprehensive renewal of the educational system and not merely tinkering with a few structural changes in the regulatory bodies such as the University Grants Commission or the All India Council for Technical Education. This book speculates on the perspective that has to develop and the supporting system to sustain it. The book does not provide a blueprint of the proposed system because this would depend on the acceptance of the perspective itself.

From speeches in the British Parliament at the time the educational system was devised, and subsequent writings on the subject, the present system was designed for a different social purpose—primarily to provide lower level manpower to the rapidly developing British trade and commerce, and the requirements of the then government in India. While the institutional framework in broad terms was modeled after the educational system in the United Kingdom, the content depended on the perceived needs of the society. Significant changes in the system of education were made after Indian independence, but many of these changes were initiated outside the university system by creating institutions of excellence such as CSIR network of research laboratories, Institutes of Technology, Indian Institutes of Management, etc. Because they were removed from the university system which has many functions and areas to provide general education, they tended to serve the immediate need of a profession without linking education with society as a whole. Notwithstanding the fact that the university system has produced some outstanding individuals, as a system they have failed to serve the purpose of knowledge creation. The university system in the United Kingdom, which provided a model for similar systems in India, are now themselves changing rapidly. The Oxford and the Cambridge universities are in the process of developing systems to compete with Harvard and Yale in the USA In our case we must look at our own situation and develop knowledge-base for a dynamic society. I believe that for this purpose models need not necessarily be based on countries abroad. As an example, Gurukul pattern of education or Nalanda which in their time served the needs of the society might show a direction at least in term of teaching methodology, teacher-student relationship, the knowledge creating environment and many such aspects that characterise a highly creative institution.

What should University Education Achieve?

Educational institutions, as other organisations in society, are created to serve a specific function—to provide knowledge, prepare individuals to serve a productive and meaningful life, and reflect on how social systems, institutions, etc. remain dynamic: All these institutions exist because the society provides sustenance. Business has markets, support for products and services; Cultural institutions provide refinements in life which are again sustained by society. The institutions so created keep the society dynamic. There is interdependence between institutions and society each deriving energy from the other. The role of an educational institution, including a university, should be identified in this overall framework. Swami Vivekanand had said: "We want that education by which character is formed, strength of mind increased, the intellect is expanded, and by which one can stand on ones' own feet." This quotation, I believe, provides the end-goal of education and also shows a link between education and society.

Primarily, an educational institution or a university in a society has to perform the following three functions:

1. Education should provide a knowledge base in soft, hard and technical areas including the emerging areas of knowledge that provide futuristic perspectives.
2. Institutionally and at the individual level generate new knowledge and applications.
3. Disseminate relevant knowledge for the benefit of individuals, policy-making and institutions in society.

Education should help students sharpen their life-goals, and ability to critically evaluate decision on matters relating to events around them. They should be able to develop sensitivity to people and situations and work with them. What was relevant in earlier times may no longer be relevant in the modern context on account of large numbers seeking education, subject specialisation, technological inputs, etc. but the Gurukul and Nalanda system did highlight many important aspects of the educational process. It shows direction for understanding people, tolerance, learner-teacher relationship as important components of the educational process. Such factors contribute to the maturing of an individual, and one's roles and responsibility as a citizen. How such aspects can be built into the educational system is our challenge as educationist and policy-makers.

Each of the aspects mentioned above need further elaboration:

Educational Function

A student opts to take up education at the university level and chooses an area of study. A number of students seek admission because without a university degree jobs are difficult to find. The existing vocational courses have not gained wide acceptance. The educational system has as yet not developed an adequate range of career-specific programmes. This is primarily due to the fact that until recently there have been limited job opportunities. The choice of subjects or the area by a student is invariably based on suggestions of parents, co-students, or personal considerations, and rarely on the basis of informed knowledge about careers. Many students get into an educational stream and later take up positions which are far removed from their subject of study. The educational system should provide scope to a student to choose courses of study and through this experience, decide on what he/she likes and enjoys. When a student has to think and choose subjects the probability is high that a larger number of them will have the urge to read, talk to others who come from different streams, and apply themselves. In the present system most students take up a course to pass an examination, rather than exercise the curiosity to learn the subject. In this respect the American University System allows considerable choice to students. As a student in Engineering faculty, I was required to do a certain number of credits in engineering subjects and I could take a number of subjects in literature, philosophy, history in other faculties. The credits from these courses were counted for graduation in engineering. While choosing a course in other areas I had to talk to a lot of people in these faculties to find out about the subject, the teaching quality of the teacher and look at several courses from which to choose. This exercise helped me to contact and interact with people who had different perspectives than mine. It helped me to broaden my social awareness and also develop friendships.

The Indian system of choosing a professional group of subjects is too rigid and confining. At best it caters exclusively to the subject knowledge rather than developing the person as an individual. The system is not student-friendly. Even the new universities in India are following the 'we know what is good for you' approach rather than one based on 'we believe that you must choose your life-goal and life-interest and we have a range of subjects/areas that can help you to prepare for it.' Most universities abroad where I studied had advisers among the faculty with whom one could discuss the choice of courses, or any other academic matters. In India most students have to discuss their concerns with individuals who have inadequate knowledge of the system. In a large number of cases, the university system does not make any serious demands on teachers to continuously update their knowledge. Some do so from their own urge to acquire knowledge. While on paper the requirement of publications and academic contribution is laid down for promotion of teachers most such stipulations are overlooked in several cases due to unspecified circumstances. As a member of the promotion committee for full professorship in a well-established university, one associate professor was recommended for promotion. The person concerned had written a few articles for newspapers on general subjects, had done no research in his area of specialisation or published anything significant but the Head of the concerned department strongly supported his case because he said that he is a very good person and due to retire in a year. The promotion would qualify him for higher pension on retirement. In my experience this was not an isolated case. Absence of academic outputs by faculty rarely encourage students to undertake serious and continuous study. They study their textbooks just before examination time, and hardly anything besides. The knowledge-base of graduates in most areas of study is woefully inadequate. This is reflected in technical courses as well. Some students do well in spite of the system. These are exceptions.

Motive for Choice of Profession

Around 30/40 years ago teachers chose the profession of teaching and learning. Like some other professionals such as those in banking, medicine, law, etc. they were respected for their integrity and the knowledge and expertise they gave to the society. This social status of most professionals has diffused largely because of their goals having shifted from service to personal economic well-being, or personal power through political affiliation, or by chasing a position of authority. This observation is not to censure the practise, or value-based. It is meant to highlight that the environment of the educational system and the symbols of success have shifted from academic achievement to personal wealth, and personal goals. This shift was initiated and led by professional programmes such as management, architecture, medicine, law and others, and has more or less covered most faculties in the educational system. Whether it is good or bad is a different issue and needs separate consideration. The relevance of this circumstance is that the focus has shifted from knowledge-creation to personal or monetary gain in most departments, more specially the one's concerned with professional education. The consequence of this shift is that priorities of teachers have shifted from in-depth study, research, teaching to devising ways of obtaining additional income.

The university system should nurture an environment of inquiry, an urge to understand the "why" and "how" of whatever they observe and not take things for granted. The student should understand the social reality of the society in which he/she lives.

The system should encourage students to understand their role in society and develop their life-goals through interactions with fellow students, faculty, studies, etc. Not all students may fully apply themselves to serve the goals of education but if the educational institutions do not develop systems and practices that encourage students to strive towards such goals, the probability is high that education will not serve its primary purpose, and it will fail to contribute towards society what it is meant to do. If the university educational system does not provide a foundation for this to happen, the dream of knowledge society would remain a distant dream.

A highly regarded teacher in management, Douglas McGregor, had highlighted that the assumptions underlying a policy guides the actions that we take. An underlying assumption that people like to shirk work would lead to a policy of close supervision of work of employees. The McGregor thesis suggests that observed behaviour of people about shirking work may be a reaction to the supervisory practice and not an inherent characteristic of the nature of men. On the contrary, an assumption that people like to work when given a certain facilitating environment would lead to an action plan by management for creating conditions that would encourage people to work (McGregor, 1960). In literature this is referred to as self-fulfilling prophecy. In educational planning, if the goal is one of developing a person as a person, the system would evolve policies, practices, teaching methodology, student-teacher relationship, etc. that would support the idea, and probability is high that many students would respond to the system. If the educational planning fails to put individual growth in focus and lacks policies and practices to support this concern, the probability is high that the desired result will not be achieved. One of the problems in our educational system is that we believe that students come with the motive of getting a degree which would qualify him/her for a job. This is perhaps true. At the same time there is little attempt on the part of a large number of institutions and teachers to develop teaching methodologies that would excite students to become interested in learning. In many institutions we refer to them as "*Baccha*" (children) and often treat them as such. We spoon feed them in studies; hand hold them in a variety of ways; rarely insist on keeping schedules and discipline, etc. We need to review this conception. All of us as teachers have seen students who begin to recognise the value of learning. In this change teachers play a significant role.

One student who came back after studying english literature from a university in the UK for one year responded to my question of what he liked most about his study compared to his earlier experience in India, by saying 'freedom to study on one's own' also implying that they treat students as 'adults'.

In the past a university has always been seen as a centre for learning and knowledge-creation. The introduction of technical education, diffused over time, this focus. The older universities such as Oxford and Cambridge in the UK and many others still value liberal education but developments in business and increasing pressure on public services have shifted the emphasis away from broad-based education to what are referred to as 'job-related' courses. When I attended an Advance Management Programme in early 60's many teachers prescribed reading material from classical literature, philosophy and related subjects. In the last 25 years or so the subject specialisation appears to have driven the 'non-technical' material out of technical education. In recent years, however, this concern has been raised in many forums concerned with education.

Education must also have its roots in the culture and tradition of society. If it is not so, the students may learn but it is unlikely that they would emotionally become a part of the educational system, and absorb fully its goals and objectives. Many educationists believe that if the early years of education are not in local language, students do absorb words but do not become a part of the system. However, the educational system must be a part of society but in some ways remain also distant from it to be able to influence societal change and dynamism.

The complex and different nature of task-demands in university require an administrative system which promotes innovation, uses diversity to advantage, inspires confidence of institutional members, and sensitivity to people and situations. The management of an academic institution is basically different from that of business, government and public systems. We have had outstanding leaders in universities but due to rapid expansion of universities, the established traditions have been lost. The problem is generally recognised but little action is taken to correct it.

The Academic Programme

The academic programme should be flexible as it is in the university system in the United States. The setting up of departments/areas of knowledged creation have to be guided by the following considerations:

1. Subject/discipline may have to follow its own requirements. For example, hard sciences such as physics, chemistry, biology, etc. have strong linkages with laboratory, but soft sciences such as psychology, sociology, political science, etc. have greater societal links. The methodology of knowledge pursuit in these areas are likely to be different. Technology and engineering may have yet another approach. Hence the organisational design of each area and evaluation criteria, examination requirements, etc. should be consistent with the requirements of concerned areas.
2. Besides these traditional departments/areas of knowledge-creation, the emergence of application-oriented, and integration of subject-areas has

critical importance for knowledge advancement. For example, bio-technology or bio-engineering, application of life sciences, environment, and a large number of such areas draw concepts from several disciplines and subjects. They also derive knowledge from operating organisations and develop a language of their own. The centres that require contribution from many different areas of study, and application, require dedicated research teams drawn from different areas, close collaboration with organisations engaged in operations, policy-makers and many other concerned people. In many applied areas of study, knowledge creation and application are simultaneous processes, and would require somewhat different administrative framework or support than those engaged primarily in the study of an academic discipline or subject.

3. The departments/areas would have to collaborate with other departments, and students would have to acquire subject knowledge in many related area. The university would have to follow a system of assigning credits for each course depending on the work-load and any other agreed criteria. Each department would require a total number of credits to graduate at either undergraduate or post graduate levels in the department. The student would be required to take, say 70 per cent courses in the assigned courses and the balance in other Faculties

under advise from his concerned supervisor. For example, a student registered to graduate in physics would be required to take 70 per cent courses in the physics faculty and the remaining 30 per cent in arts, literature or whatever other areas that he/she chooses. Credits earned by the student in these courses would be added to the aggregate required to graduate in physics faculty.

4. Two courses however should be compulsory for students irrespective of the faculty in which he/she is registered for a degree. The courses are:
   (i) The history of independence movement in India
   (ii) Culture, Art and Literature of India

The purpose of these two compulsory courses is that students should begin to see the foundation that binds our society. Culture and tradition contribute to the quality of life in the society. While globalisation relates to trade and commerce, and in conception attempts to provide equal opportunity to countries to operate in the global environment by instituting regulatory and negotiatory mechanisms, the exchanges among nations opens up doors for communication and interaction among countries, different cultures and traditions. Such exchanges should develop mutual understanding for a wide range of values and sensibilities among countries. Our society values family, tolerance, spirituality (something beyond oneself), etc. which have contributed immensely, and continue to contribute, to the one-ness of the Indian nation (Kakar and Kakar, 2007). It is appropriately mentioned in one advertisement that 'Times change. Our values don't'. The educational system should encourage among students the understanding and the rationale of both globalised systems and the ethos that bind our society.

Student in art and commerce subjects should be encouraged to take subjects like history of science and technology. These subjects are necessary to prevent a myopic perspective of the subject in which the student is pursuing his/her primary subject/discipline. Education should be broad-based.

The university should also arrange some credits for students of some or all subjects to take up social service in rural areas. Likewise the university should encourage students to develop entrepreneurial ventures for which they can receive credit in their programme. The grade could depend on the quality of the project and its defense by the student.

5. Each academic area or unit would have to prepare a detailed annual activity plan to include the academic plan of each member of the faculty; collective tasks of the unit concerned should be reviewed by its Academic Committee or Council, which would consist of the head, 3 or 4 members of the faculty,

2/3 members of another faculty in the university and 4/6 members appointed by the university. The council would approve the plans and review progress at suitable intervals. In the present context of limited research output, the council will help the university system to promote research awareness, and its relevance to the society and the social institutions. Every three years the unit or the university would undertake audit of the quality of work undertaken. Work planning at individual and collective levels provides direction and leaves enough scope for individuals to pursue their areas of interest. Having said this, academic freedom should not mean that a person can choose to contribute nothing. Freedom should mean that one can pursue his chosen area of work to excell in his own knowledge-base.

6. Special attention is necessary to evolve a teaching methodology that would serve the purpose of the course as visualized by the teacher (Dayal, 2007).

The Role of the Teacher in the University

The progression of teachers should depend upon the quality of their contribution in teaching, research, publications, consulting or any task specially assigned to the individual concerned. The university would have to lay down minimum standards to have a planning system which can provide sufficient choice to a teacher to follow areas of his/her interests. In an academic institution, the institutional management has to evolve a balance between institutional requirements on the one hand and the individual's need to pursue his own area of specialisation on the other. In applied areas of study this equation is more complex because a teacher has to acquire familiarity with other related areas and cooperate with others in many projects. The academic community would have to evolve codes and standards for carrying out accountability to the institution, the peers, the duly constituted authority in the institution, the students and the society that supports the educational system.

Institutional Leadership

The demands on institutional leadership in an educational institution are varied. One significant factor is that the responsibility for the nature and quality of the programme is primarily determined and carried out by the faculty where the institutional leadership has little direct role except one of facilitating the process. The assessment of the quality of input is complex. The institutional leadership has to employ a range of motivational approaches to generate among members of the faculty a concern for continuously develop subject specialisation and at the same time, a spirit of working together. These roles are distinct, not complementary.

The leader derives his authority through his/her acceptance as a person by the institutional community, and not merely by formal powers assigned to the position by higher authority. The quality of output depends on this relationship, especially in the Indian context. Each member of the faculty has a different motive to take up a position, and his/her expectations from the institution are influenced by his/her needs. Unlike in a business organisation, the institutional leader would have to treat each individual as a separate entity. This is so because the focus in a business situation is on the product, the market, and an individual has to develop the capability to devise the best fit between his approach and the market situation. In an academic situation the individual himself is the focus—he is the creator as well the deliverer and the institution relies on his contribution to sustain itself. Each individual's creativity depends on a variety of considerations including his sense of belonging and the environment of creativity that the leadership generates.

The institutional demands on its leadership in the Western situation are considerably different from the Indian. In the West the emphasis is on the task and faculty take up academic positions by choice. The faculty is self-motivated and are liable to loose their position if they fail to perform their institutional tasks. In India, relationships lead to task performance. Having made the point about differences in respect to leader demands in the West and India, there is a great deal of decentralisation in the West in respect to academic tasks through several committee structures. Most committees in the academic context in India rarely work as a committee. Members do not devote time and attention to the committee except when they have some vested involvement in some aspect of its work. Consequently, committees rarely complete their work on schedule and keep asking for extension of date for submission of the report. We have to evolve ways of involving people in academic tasks. The need for this exercise is necessary. It is most doubtful that academic committees as they now function serve their intended purpose. Some institutions have addressed this problem by creating strong peer culture among the faculty. This does not happen without a deliberate plan to do so. Indian Institute of Management, Ahmedabad is able to do so. The processes of achieving this kind of institutional culture are available in literature (Dayal, 2006; Mathhai, 1977).

References

Dayal, I (2008). *Teaching of Management*, Ane Books India, New Delhi.

Dayal, I (2006). *Early Years of IIMA* in Deepak Dogra, (Ed.) Ishwar Dayal on Management, Vol. III, Ane Books India, New Delhi.

Kakar, S and Kakar, K (2007). *The Indians, Portait of a People,* Penguin, New Delhi.

Mathhai, R, Pareek, U and Roo, T V (1977). *The Institution Building in Education and Research*, All India Management Association, New Delhi.

McGregor, D (1960). *The Human Side of Enterprise*, McGraw-Hill, New York.

2

Higher Education—Through the Ages

Somonnoy Ghosh

The paper surveys the historical and socio-economic underpinnings of higher education in the world and the purpose it is serving, with special reference to our country. In India, with state regulated systems where often bureaucracy and ministries have had a greater say than apolitical educationists, on one hand, and rampant privatization of higher education in certain sectors on the other, one can not help but think that something has gone deeply wrong, somewhere.

Our foray into higher education was formalized immediately after Independence with the Dr. Radhakrishnan Commission laying down the role of higher education in the years to come. In his report, Dr.Radhakrishnan emphasized: "Democracy depends

---

Somonnoy Ghosh is Director Development at Indus World School of Business, Greater Noida, U.P. This paper was written by him on request of the author.

for its very life on a high standard of general, vocational and professional education. Dissemination of learning, incessant search for new knowledge, unceasing effort to plumb the meaning of life, provision of professional education to satisfy occupational needs of our society are the vital tasks of higher education." Dr. Kothari who headed the Commission set up in 1964 echoed his sentiments. The Kothari Commission Report, in 1966, stated: "'The role of education is to improve the material standard of people and to enrich quality of life. Besides knowledge and skills, education should be also concerned with the 'inner content' of our lives, with ideas and idealism and strengthening of the spirit."

Alas, almost a decade down into the third millennium we are grappling with issues of executing their vision and have perhaps moved even farther from the ideals envisaged by our forefathers. It must be mentioned here that one is by no means decrying the numerical growth in the number of higher education colleges and centres, and in the number of graduates and postgraduates being produced by them. Numerically, although far below many of our Western and Asian counterparts in terms of the Gross Enrollment Ratio, we are not doing too badly. Where we seem to have lost our way significantly is that somehow we have forgotten a vital purpose of education – that of "enriching the quality of life" or, that of egging learners to deal with questions related to the "meaning of life", both in the context of the self, and the society.

One is also well aware of the counterargument that the role and purpose of higher education must change to adapt to the needs of the hour. And this is apparently what has happened, by and large, if one goes by how higher education has evolved historically.

The first practice of organised education that was meant to serve specific purpose for the society can be traced back to the 5th century BC Athens. At almost the same time India saw the emergence of its first University at Nalanda. In the true sense of the word, the University at Nalanda saw the convergence of scholars from different parts of the world to its residential campus to study and discourse on almost all areas/ disciplines prevalent at that time. There was rich exchange of ideas and philosophies amongst these scholars reinforcing an open learning culture.

Historians contend that the idea of a liberal education in Athens originated in response to the culture conflicts that made the citizens explore the character of a democratic culture. Athens, at the time, was symbolic of a developing democracy where most decisions were made in an assembly of debating citizens.

The Athenian society was divided into two classes – the free and the slaves. Both had well-defined roles. Whereas the slaves were expected to be adept at handling crafts, trade and business, and were sometimes better at it than their masters, the latter, on the other hand, were expected to involve themselves in the rights and duties of a free citizen – participating in debates in the assembly, in the jury system, and war. Ergo, the education mostly focused on equipping these "free" citizens with special skills, *technai*, so that they could function more effectively as free people. This education was in fact the new flavour, having transformed from the older, more literary order that largely emphasized memorization of ancient texts.

It might be interesting to note that the new skills embraced by the Athenians included rhetoric, grammar and logic – essentially the ability to speak articulately, and persuasively – skills that were hammered out of the need for a society to create a democratic culture.

This liberal character of education, which was anchored on the civic needs of the society, however, was eventually lost after the conquests of Alexander and later with the advent of the Roman domination. While on the face of it, the elements of education remained quite the same as earlier, its use was vastly different – it was used by the new populations of Syrians, Egyptians and the likes in the Mediterranean basin to "Hellenize" so as to climb the social ladder and achieve economic advancement.

In essence, the liberal foundations of education that upheld the civic character of the Greek society eventually gave way to a more economically utilitarian form owing to a different need of the times.

Later, during the era of Christianity, higher education was much influenced by the Church. Theology, which had its roots in the Greek culture and the Roman period was the order of the day, and necessarily so for the *ekklesia* to preserve classical literature. Alas, unlike the period in the 5th century Athens, higher education had become elitist to serve the purpose of the leadership.

If we turn our attention to early America, post the civil revolution, the American schools decided to follow the traditional curriculum borrowed from Cambridge and Oxford that emphasised on ancient classics, rhetoric, Christian ethics and philosophy. Needless to say, the purpose was to create leaders for the Church, various offices and the society.

The industrial revolution saw various nations and their system of education adapt to the new demands of nation building through industrialization. The emphasis shifted to the application of engineering and technology to produce goods, as well as to research in these areas, in addition to others such as agriculture. Perhaps no other nation responded to the industrial revolution more arduously as America, where we saw the emergence of new educational structures. Traditional liberal arts subjects were gradually replaced by the more modern disciplines of arts and sciences. American colleges also adopted the system of majoring in a discipline through studying of elective courses.

If the industrial revolution was responsible for the adoption by the world of a more vocational character of higher education, it was the World War I, followed by the World War II, which really catalysed the focus of education onto engineering, technology and medicine, and other areas of vocation and trade. Post World War II, in America there arose a debate between two groups – one that wanted to revert to the traditional curriculum of studying the classical texts and religion, and the other, that of "American pragmatists," that wanted the academic community to respond to the developmental needs of the American democratic society by engaging in studies that required experimentation and collection and analysis of empirical evidence.

We all know which way did America move, and how, with time, a fairly extensive democratisation of higher education took place. Similar shifts happened elsewhere in the world, especially in Europe, although the latter did manage to retain some essence of the traditional education system that had emerged in England and a few other nations centuries ago.

So we find ample evidence of how higher education has time and again evolved world over in keeping with the changing times and needs.

Coming back to the present context, and to India in specific, let us examine the state of higher education and the basis of my statement that much may not be right.

As noted earlier, with the proliferation of higher education institutions and colleges, be they largely private, the absolute numbers do not look bad at all. For example, with over 2.5 million graduates produced every year, India is amongst the top three countries in the world on this count. Or, the 350,000 odd engineers that we produce every year far outscores the number produced in America. Some of our centres of higher learning are believed to be of very high standard – be they the IITs, or the AIIMS, or the National Law Schools, or the IIMs.

In the recent years our strength in certain areas has been acknowledged by the world. India is looked upon as a country that is likely to ride on the new knowledge economy wave. Our engineers and scientists are doing very fine work the world over. Then how do we say that things have not gone right for Indian higher education?

Well, experts contend that even though this is the case there is much to be desired. Even though our absolute numbers are high they fall pitiably short of the desired numbers for a country of India's size and population. If we are to reach anywhere near the target number of universities set by the National Knowledge Commission, we cannot afford to stick to our "one size fits all" policy. We must evolve a far more decentralised and autonomous system that encourages excellence through adoption of world-class standards, through accreditation and self-regulation.

While our think tank and policy-makers concern themselves with the question of growth in the number of universities and centres of higher learning in India, we all seem to be readying ourselves to leverage upon the opportunity presented by an "ageing" world that will need huge numbers of knowledge workers in the coming decades – a need which India presumably can fulfill with its relatively young and huge population.

But in our preoccupation with numbers and scale we seem to be grossly missing out on one critical aspect – we are confusing professional and technical education with general education. As a result, earning a degree or a diploma that enhances our employability is often equated to getting a good education. Nothing could, however, be farther from the truth.

Incidentally, the word university derived from the Latin *universitas*, literally means the whole universe, or more contextually, the coming together of a large number of disciplines and faculty to create, share and disseminate knowledge. Many of these disciplines are general in the sense that they do not necessarily create attributes desired by employers – such as philosophy, history, literature, arts, theatre, cinema, and so on. These disciplines have been collectively termed as liberal arts in the United States, and have been witnessing an alarming drop in the number of enrollments the world over. With rising cost of education, the question being asked by learners and students most frequently today is

– what is the return on their investment? Naturally, getting a degree is often seen as a means to a paying career, and only that.

And it is this question which is increasingly determining the choice of discipline by students all over the world. In India, the word career has become synonymous with money and perks and social status. Millions of students each year are running harder to seek the big opportunities on offer by competing to enroll themselves in the "best" of schools. Those who can not get into the best are contending by opting for the second, or the third, or the fourth best – *ad infinitum.* And just look at the ramifications of this mad race. Not only are students and their parents spending large sums of money with unscrupulous coaching centres that promise excellent results, the so-called world of opportunities is causing much anxiety and social stress. Even the colleges are vying with each other in "selling" their programmes on the basis of the placement records.

I was recently reading a newspaper article that reported that the good colleges of the Delhi University now have their own placement cells and the fresh graduates from these colleges are offered jobs by some of the most popular recruiters. It is a different matter that the jobs offered have little bearing on what they may have formally learned during their undergraduate programmes.

On one hand one can argue that these are positive signs reflective of the huge growth phase that our country is going through. Isn't it only good that the fruits of the growing job market are percolating down to the more regular colleges and universities? On the other hand one wonders whether the purpose of education can be so narrowed down as to only serve the needs of the growing industry. What will be next? Are we going to witness recruiters lining up outside higher secondary schools? The idea may not be all that preposterous. After all, aren't school leaving children bright enough to be trained on the job?

The return on investment is a worrying concern even from the perspective of those who are investing in creating education infrastructures and resources, especially the private bodies. We have ventured into a phase when quantification of output and results is taking away from the critical significance of the more intangible qualitative characteristics of the society that our fathers of democracy had dreamed about. Well, isn't it far simpler to measure the utility of education by the wealth it generates for society? The question is, in the long run is it only wealth that will determine the well being of society, or the quality of life?

This is precisely the primary point that I am trying to make. We have been going through a phase of societal transformation – one that has been impacting our lives very quietly but definitively. This transformation is slow and may not be very directly visible, but it is there all the same. It is causing our society to become more result oriented – quick results, sometimes in total disregard to the means, more competitive, less accommodating, less egalitarian. And yes, it is making us intolerant and impatient and often uncooperative. Our forefathers certainly did not bargain for these as fruits of education.

So, what exactly is causing this departure from the stated goals of Dr. Radhakrishnan and Dr. Kothari, or Tagore and Gandhi? Let me cite a few cases to make my point. The 5-year flagship programme of the National Law School of India University at Bangalore has only two courses on Sociology, a couple more on Political Science, and none on Psychology. The rest are hardcore law courses. The 2-year flagship MBA programme at IIM Ahmedabad teaches only one course on "Indian Social and Political Environment" – the rest are of course hardcore business related courses. The IITs seem to fare somewhat better even though their mandate is to produce engineers and technologists. At most IITs, an undergraduate student has to register for at least 4 to 5 courses in Humanities and Social Sciences. At IIT, Kanpur I took courses as diverse as Philosophy, Psychology and Modern Art, amongst others.

Our educators and the ones who decide on the curricula have somehow missed a vital point – that while we must create professionals who are competent in their fields, in the process we are also creating individuals who are shaping up the society. Any organisation is also a part of the society and the culture, attitudes and values we set in organisations are also going to impact these attributes in the society of which the organisations are a part. If the society comprises largely of silo-ed individuals who know little besides their work, how can we expect to build a society that is humane, creative, diverse in its outlook, and sensitive to the common values of sharing and participation that created the society in the first place?

To conclude, I would like to urge the policy-makers and educators in our country to go beyond quantitative measures of output of education, to recognise the slow but steady departure we are making from the visions of our forefathers, and to instill appreciation amongst students about the myriad wonders of this world, including human beings and cultures, by including more of the liberal arts courses into any curricula. After all, wouldn't we like our lawyers, doctors, engineers and managers to be model citizens of this country?

3

University and Society

I begin my examination with the question whether the role of a university in a society which is in transition is somewhat more comprehensive than it is in the West which has provided a model for our university system, and we often compare the two to evaluate our own. As discussed in the earlier chapter; the university has a distinct responsibility to the society in which it exists. In the West, the primary responsibility is to generate knowledge and ways of transmitting it to those who may use it. I believe that in a society in transition the additional responsibility of educational institutions has to be to also contribute towards development of a person as a person. I refer to this function as 'citizen role'.

In nearly 50 years of my association with students at the postgraduate level, I have found that many young people have problems of adjustment to changing demand, confusion about their relationships with one or both parents, a sense of drift and uncertainty about themselves, and anger. Some of them take on asocial habits which, ultimately grip them (Garg and Parikh, 1993).

In the institutions with which I have been associated, we encouraged easy access to faculty for students to discuss their personal problems but there are likely to be many who bottle up their anxiety which often leads to further anger without knowing the root of it. There is a sense of helplessness among many managers at all levels even when they have individually achieved success. To a large extent the diminishing bonds of family, the sense of belonging, and the unconditional support of the family have contributed to increased anxiety levels. Only a few organisations provide conditions that could substitute the feelings of support or belonging that earlier patterns of family environment provided. This is the dilemma that many young people experience in most traditional societies in transition. In contrast, the primary socialisation in the United States develops independence and individualism which is reinforced in corporate life. They experience intra-person conflict as against inter-social conflicts that individuals experience in India. However, a number of young people with weakening family bonds show signs of intra-person problems. In many cases they have not developed the capability to resolve them on their own.

There is another characteristic of the Indian situation. With rare exceptions the schools in India are concerned with book-learning and little that contributes to personal growth or a sense of accepting responsibility for oneself. When I was a postgraduate student in New York in late 1940s, I worked as a research associate in Columbia University in New York on a project called 'Citizenship Education'. General D. Eisenhower who was President of Columbia University at that time had personally initiated the project. It was an action-research project to understand how best citizenship could be taught in schools. My research group was concerned with an elaborate exercise to evaluate effectiveness of teaching citizenship in select schools. A great deal of literature had also come out on related subjects in the 1950s. The President of the United States had also set up leaders of largest corporations and known individuals in society to bring out a volume on 'Goals for Americans' (1960). Schools were widely concerned about the subject. In contrast, in the school to which I went in India, we had one period reserved for what was called 'civics' in those days. I hardly remember what was taught in this subject. In more recent years even that is not included in the curricula in schools or colleges. I believe that in a democracy education for citizenship is important because one element of underlying strength of a democratic system is that individuals have a significant role in making the system effective. They have to exercise their rights and discharge their obligations with knowledge and understanding of its implications.

These aspects of our societal characteristics are important to recognise because the educational system has to play a significant role in value-creation and societal transformation. In view of the changing profile of family and the environment which supported relationships and inadequate attention to such aspects in school education, the university system should be concerned with the development of people and understanding of citizenship. These concerns are based on two premises:

1. Democratic structure of governance has higher probability of achieving equitable societal framework than any other known structured systems of governance. As a young man I had read with fascination Jai Prakash Narain's book called *Why Socialism*. It had caught my fancy in my late teens. However, I am now convinced that no system with highly centralized power-base can achieve an equitable society. This is because it has in-built scope to give in to greed for power and regulating the will of the leadership on citizens by one means or another. This is as true in governance of a nation as that of work organisations. Having said this, no system can produce results expected of it without creating structures and a mechanism to support the system. Equally important is a review mechanism and checks and balances that flash signals of deviate action. These have to be created in both educational systems and societal organisations.

I believe that democracy needs strong institutions that can express their views without fear or reprisal, and people who can work beyond their personal interests: the educational system including university has a significant role in developing such people.

2. The educational system should provide the citizens an understanding of democratic rights and obligations including citizen role in a democracy. An idea or an ideal is an abstract notion. It can only be realised by formulating a systematic plan of action. The developing knowledge in social sciences provide direction for planning relevant action plans to achieve a goal or an idea. Things do not happen on their own. An idea has little meaning without a plan of action to realise it. The democratic structure and promise of an equitable society requires institutional support and citizen awareness to achieve the stated goal.

University for Education

There are many people who contend that a university is for knowledge creation and teaching, as some businessmen claim that business of business is business. Neither propositions are valid. All institutions are interdependent on one another. The cumulative effect of all these contribute to the forming of a national identity. Globalisation has to do with free interaction for trade and commerce and a network that could, at least in its concept, provide cheaper goods and services, and contribute to quality of life of all people. This hasn't happened so far. The quality of life depends not only in respect to availability of goods and a wide range of services but, in essence, emotional well-being as well as a sense of belonging, being wanted, and a network of relationships. These aspects relate to the societal ethos which in turn affects all institutions. Globalisation, even in its conceptual frame, does not minimise the societal role. I believe that a strong national identity is necessary for global networks to work. The notion of networking requires equality among players or members constituting the network, and not abject dependence of one on the other. Likewise the business, the educational system, the political and other sub-systems have to acquire strength by cooperative stance, and not by drawing discrete boundaries around themselves. Business, education, public and other systems cannot function without deriving support from one another. In this scenario education as other sub-system is concerned with ways of preparing individuals who are emotionally adjusted to their environment. In conceptualising the rationale and function of the educational system, a university has to be concerned with developing a person as a person, besides the role of knowledge-creation and dissemination.

Sudhir Kakar, the noted psychoanalyst, writer and teacher in his interview published in *The Hindu* dated

August 18, 2008 said that the biggest mistake we are committing is to discourage our children's power of imagination. This is one of the biggest problems of our educational system. For any reorientation of the educational system, which is imperative for the quality of life in its comprehensive meaning, we need to cross the self-created barriers of providing book learning, not education. This concern has to be reflected in the teaching methodology, course planning and student-teacher relationship. In some of the better known universities with which I have had closer contact, a large number of teachers share this concern. Many of them spend a fair amount of time with students. However, these interactions in most cases are around the subject matter. This is partially so because the function of the university is seen as that of knowledge provider.

The Administrative Support and Organisational Structure

Most institutions in India have a high degree of centralisation of authority and power. The total organisation revolves around an individual. When the incumbent in this position changes, the new person, more often than not, gives a new twist to the direction and functions. For example, one vice-chancellor, in a personal interaction, mentioned that under his stewardship only merit and performance of an academic is considered for promotion to higher teaching positions. He mentioned that his predecessor was more liberal in these matters. He gave many examples of changes he initiated with a view to upgrading the academic performance of the departments in the university. His successor does not show the same enthusiasm and has different approaches and concerns. This is not an isolated experience of one university but prevails in many others. The university system is constantly in a state of flux.

The formal organisation, on paper, provides checks and balances built into the system. The executive committee, for example, is concerned with major policies. In most places it is highly politicised. The deans in departments have considerable autonomy in respect to departmental matters but they have to depend, in most cases, on the larger decision-making bodies. For example, they cannot take independent decisions about introducing new programmes. They have to seek approvals on many financial and academic matters, and are bound by more or less inflexible rules and regulations. It is rare to find that in a large and complex organisation such decision-making remains free of politicisation within the system. Most system- related decisions are governed by alignments forged by individuals within the system (Dayal, 1992; Abid Hussain, 1986). In the review of the inhibiting factors in the university system, it is necessary to examine the way it operates and not what is laid down in a manual. The operating system is what influences performance and behaviour of people in an organisation. The formal organisation represents the intended pattern.

The widely prevailing system of affiliating colleges with the university may have been meaningful many years ago but I wonder if this arrangement serves any meaningful purpose in the present context. The centralised examination and grading arrangement has been the subject of a great deal of discussion and criticism. In fact centralisation of control in almost all spheres of activity develops power-based systems, and leads to demonstrable laxity in quality and responsibility at both institutional and individual levels. It is most unlikely that innovation and creativity could become a hallmark of the educational institutions without removing known roadblocks from the educational system. Regulatory bodies such as UGC and AICTE have to show leadership in reforming the system and redefining their own role.

Administrative and control practices have to be evolved from the imperatives of the culture and the attitudes and sentiments prevailing in the society. Later in this book I have discussed the impact of culture and tradition on administrative practices in Chapters 7 and 8.

The University-Society-Industry

Another issue that is seriously being discussed round the university campuses in the USA concerns the nature of relationship between the university and the industry. A university has to have a deep understanding of the society, the industry and public systems. Yet, they have to have an independent capacity to interpret problems and issues to be able to meaningfully contribute new perspectives based on independent experience, research findings and a variety of experiences. In any institutional and social environment, people develop a mental set, attitudes, interpretations, etc. They provide the mental filters through which people generally look at and interpret what they observe and hear. A few examples would illustrate the phenomenon.

I had chosen a case in a training programme for about 30 senior civil servants. After the case discussion I asked them what contributed to their interpretation and discussion. The answers to this question showed that somewhere at the back of their mind, as a group, they distrusted the private business motives and this coloured their interpretation of the situation in the case. The case used in another programme for senior business executives led to totally different interpretations based on their own mental perception. This is not a unique example. In teaching and in life these differences are explained by the phenomena referred to as organisational socialisation. A manager knows about the problem of his organisation more than a consultant who is called in from outside to help the organisation. The consultant's attribute is that he is able to look at the phenomena from a different perspective and redefine the problem. The central point for emphasis here is that a university has to have both understanding of the society and other institutions but, at the same time, hold an independent outlook.

There is a tendency on the part of the regulatory bodies for education, or large donors of funds to universities, to control and supervise or direct the institutional work. Lester and Piore (2004) refer to this growing trend and its dysfunctionality in the following quote.

> "The involvement of business people, with their commercial interests and incentives, adds a unique perspective to the conversations on campus. But if the interests of business are fully assimilated by the university participants- that is, if there is a complete merging of horizons-not only will something be lost from the conversation, but the value to industry itself will be diminished. If MIT researchers start thinking like Microsoft researchers, the university will no longer be able to add anything to Microsoft's own interpretation of the world. Its views will no longer be distinctive." (p.167)

References

Abid Hussain, (Chairman) *The fourth Review Committee of CSIR,* Government of India, 1986, New Delhi.

Dayal, I (1991). *Managing Innovation*, Concept, New Delhi.

Dayal, I (2005). *Management Education* in Dogra, D (Ed.) *Management Education—Issues and Predilections*, Excel Books.

Garg, P K and Parikh, I J (1993). *Young Managers at the Crossroads*, Sage Publications, New Delhi.

Goals for Americans, *The Report of the President's Commission on National Goals*, A Spectrum Book, 1960, Prentice-Hall, New York.

Lester, R and Piore, M J (2004). *Innovation—The Missing Dimension*, Harvard University Press, Cambridge, Massachusetts.

4

Creativity as Institutional Culture

Creativity and innovation are the lifeblood of universities that are highly regarded for their academic performance. They are greatly respected for their contribution to knowledge and publications based on research. These achievements may be attributable to individuals who are, in a large measure, encouraged by the environment of work and supporting systems created by the university. Sustained creativity and innovation require deliberate action by institutional management for building such systems and promoting an environment for creative inputs. Many studies and research findings have identified critical conditions that promote creativity and innovation. This chapter highlights some of the research findings in the following two areas :

1. The processes that encourage creativity and innovation
2. The organisational and managerial practices that promote creativity

Creativity and innovation are considered to be two different phenomena. The report of the National Advisory Committee for Creative and Cultural Education (NACCCE), in 1999, defined creativity as below:

"Imaginative activity fashioned so as to produce outcomes that are both original and of value."

Innovation is variously viewed. However, a widely accepted view is that innovation consists of something new and original such as a product, a service, or an idea that has commercial application. However, the processes and conditions that generate both creativity and innovation in an organisation are the same. This being so, for this chapter, both are considered together.

The Process Involved in Creativity

Creativity is a process in so far as it does not suddenly happen. Before an artist puts his brush on the canvas, some image, however vague, lurk for a while at the back of his mind; something that he observes or hears and as if in a flash that image assumes a form and as he puts brush to canvas, the idea takes full shape. In my own writing I have experienced something similar. Something that I read or hear in a conversation, or even an advertisement in a newspaper, stirs something in my mind though it is seldom clear. At some time, be in another context, something activates that idea and a hoard of related things flood my mind. Often I sit down with a piece of paper and begin to write down what I have in mind. Very often when I am writing, the idea becomes clearer and I throw away the paper and put down the idea in a coherent manner. For me ideas take recognisable form after re-reading what I have written. This involves several attempts at writing before the idea fully takes shape. I have heard that this sequence is not unique to me. Some of the writers who are highly regarded have mentioned that they have to generate several drafts of what they write before the job is done to their satisfaction.

Creative phenomenon does not occur in isolation, even if at some stage of the process isolation helps. Creativity does not necessarily result from logical sequential thinking. In 2006, IBM published a report of their study comprising of intensive interviews with CEOs of companies which were known for their innovation. The survey included 765 CEOs and others comprising of 20 different industries and 11 geographical regions. The Report was called *Expanding the Innovation Horizon, The Global CEO Study*. It was released by IBM Global Business Services (IBM, 2006). Identifying some common characteristics of these organisations, the report shows that organisations with high innovation had:

- An atmosphere where employees were given the opportunity to interact freely within and outside the organisation.
- Clear direction of the areas of research.
- A time frame for the project.
- A budget for the project.
- People up the ladder of hierarchy who showed continuing interest in the project, and demonstrated their interest in review meetings and in many other ways.

In a study of many research laboratories and R & D organisations, Bernstein (1988) identified the innovative process as follows:

- Individuals are chosen with extreme care and left free to walk around the laboratories and talk to people within and outside the institution.
- Individuals are given a long enough time to achieve mutually accepted results and if this doesn't happen, the individuals are moved out.
- The management exercised process and not control of the person *i.e.* whether facilities to achieve results are adequate and how they are used, etc. Individuals were left free to work

through the task as it suited them. Review is made at the peer not the administrative level.

In a recent study of innovative processes by Lester and Piore from Harvard Business School, it was found that the analytic approach is not conducive to innovation. Rather, it is the interpretative approach that is more conducive to the process. This study included in depth studies of several organisations known for their focus on innovation. In general the decision process in organisations is based on logical analysis of the situation for diagnosing and arriving at a decision. The authors posit that innovation is not based on a logical process. It requires out of the box thinking. The meanings of several disconnected thoughts, have to be interpreted to derive a new perspective, or a different meaning, which leads to a new product or a new service or a new perspective to look at whatever surrounds an organisation. An idea is generated to begin to further it and this exploration may generate new ideas by interpretation of what occurs. Logical thinking often would lead to extension of the old, not yield anything very different. Invariably, logic, by its very nature, leads to an incremental or a related idea, not one that is radically different. Most managers in organisations are socialised by training, experience and company practices to employ logic to solve problems. Innovation needs a different orientation of people who can break away from the traditional patterns of thinking. Lester and

Piore (2004) from their research study state the following:

"Analytical processes work best when alternatives are well-understood and can by clearly defined and distinguished from one another. Interpretative processes are more appropriate when the possible outcomes are unknown-when the task is to create those outcomes and determine what their properties really are..."

They further add:

> "These two ways of proceeding involve very different kinds of skills, different ways of working together, different forms of managerial control and authority, and, ultimately, different ways of thinking about the economy. And differences are not merely ones of degree." (2004, P.6)

Researchers also found that collaboration of outsiders who have a different orientation helps the innovative process. Consulting experience supports this contention. Invariably, in my own experience of consulting in organisations, I have found that as an outsider, more often than not, interpretation based on my theoretical foundation of the available data gives a new perspective which helps in identifying the critical problem areas. People within the organisation interpret the same data differently. Once the problem is defined, the direction that could lead to remedial action becomes easier.

Innovation or creativity are essential requirements of a university. Research findings are clearly suggestive of the fact that faculty members with their orientation, should be able to interpret events to evolve new directions provided this process is encouraged and legitimised by system management. For creativity to become a way of life, and characteristic of the teaching community, the management has to develop systems and practices that facilitate the process. I believe that this consideration is important for a university to perform its knowledge-creator and societal roles.

Organisational Characteristics

The innovative process and an environment of creativity requires a conducive organisational environment and supporting administrative styles. The essential characteristics of both these aspects have been extensively brought out in many reports of review committees by the Government and extensive research in India and abroad (IBM, 2006; Lester and Piore, (2004), Dayal 1991). These are briefly discussed in two sections (i) avoiding departmental boundaries, (ii) administrative support systems.

Avoiding Departmental Boundaries

Free interaction is necessary among scientists/ teachers and people in other disciplines. In most institutions departments are created for each discipline. Partly due to these boundary conditions, interactions among different disciplines becomes restrictive. Invariably in such work arrangements rivalry among departments prevents collaboration. Institutions have tried clusters consisting of individuals with different academic orientation but have interest in the same problem areas. For example, one institution had a cluster or a centre with focus on agriculture. They had another cluster on public systems, etc. Each cluster had people from different disciplines. The inter-cluster collaboration was promoted when they shared a common problem or issue Kuriloft (1963) reported a business organisation designed on the basis of self-contained work groups with considerable success. There are many such work designs that are reported in literature (De, 1984).

The Indian system values standardisation of work arrangements and strict adherence to rules and procedures. In my interviews with scientists, several among them expressed a sense of disillusionment with the rigidity of the system in their research laboratory. Two examples from interviews will illustrate the point (Dayal, 1991, p.30).

In one research laboratory one scientist mentioned the following:

> "I spent two months of the summer vacation in a university abroad, and I was able to do more work during this period than I have been able to do in last two years here..."

In another interview a medical doctor who came back after his Ph.D on cancer studies abroad said:

> "It has taken me two years to set up a research project which would have taken no more than two weeks in the university abroad, and even now I have to answer many queries and fill up many gaps and chase some more people before I can start on my project."

In the institutions to which I have been attached for several years we had no departments or divisions, nor inhibiting rules. Our institutions were not an exception in these respects but in India there are very few of this kind. Given the understanding of the innovative process, it is entirely possible that the required work-related structures in Indian institutions would need reorientation in policy perspective and practise for them to become creative and serve the role expected of them.

The Administrative Support Systems

Experience shows that innovative institutions have to promote long-term goals which are specific.

Successful institutions promote peer culture and set up mechanisms to develop and support this culture. Standards are set by faculty which are invariably more stringent than those imposed upon them by outside regulatory bodies (Dayal, 2006). The conditions necessary for peer groups to perform these tasks depend upon the beliefs of the institutional leadership and their capability to develop the supporting environment. The leader has to be low on his own power-needs and clear on his mission.

Reporting on the characteristics at Bell Laboratories, Amo Penzias, the Vice-President of Research says:

> "One of the things that people are constantly amazed at in this place is just how little short-term management there really is, just how little short-term management I get. People do not believe that nobody tells me what to do on a daily, weekly, or even a monthly basis. Occasionally, I get a little bit of 'fatherly' advice, but in the past year I do not think I have spent as much as four hours with my boss. Instead we focus on our long-range objectives." (Bernstein, 1968, p.232)

In successful innovative organisations the controls are personalised. They facilitate progress, and rarely consist of filling up lengthy forms and providing frequent progress reports. The experience and case studies suggest the following considerations:

1. There has to be flexibility in the system to accommodate individual needs and differences.
2. The system should encourage, and promote, interactions within and outside the organisation.
3. Individuals should feel free to test their ideas. Innovation does not develop in isolation. The very nature of the innovative process relies on assimilation and interpretation of observed phenomenon, not analysis or logical thinking. However the goals have to be clear with some concern for time and budget for the project.
4. Organisation of work should avoid rigidity and predetermined standardisation imposed upon the system.
5. The controls should be personalised and lead to growth and development.
6. The leader should be low on his/her own power-needs and strong in his/her beliefs relating to people and system development.
7. There has to be a recognisable reward for performance and penalty for non-performance.

University systems and institutions would have to develop, as a policy, conditions that promote creativity. Experience and research findings show that without conducive institutional support creative output is unlikely to develop.

References

Bernstein, J (1988). *Three Degrees Above Zero*, Affiliated East-West Press, New Delhi.

Dayal, I (1991). *Managing Innovation*, Concept, New Delhi.

Dayal, I (2006). *Teaching of Management*, Ane Books India, New Delhi.

Dayal, I (2006). *Early Years of IIMA* in Deepak Dogra (Ed.), Ishwar Dayal on Management, Vol.III, Ane Books India, New Delhi.

Kuriloft, A H (1963). *An Experiment in Management-Putting Theory Y to the Test*, Personnel, American Management Association, New York pp. 8-18.

Lester, R and Piore, M J (2004). *Innovation–The Missing Dimension*, Harvard University Press, Cambridge, Massachusetts.

Report on *Expanding the Innovation Horizon, The Global CEO Study*, IBM Global Business Services, 2006.

Professional Education
Focus on Management Education

5

The Management Education Scenario in India

Technical Education is not new for India. However, there is need in some areas to develop new approaches/perspectives. For my purpose I have taken management education because of my familiarity with it. My interactions with other profesional courses such as law, architecture, etc. show similar considerations as brought out in this chapter. The analysis of the educational process has to follow its historical development because at any point of time the system has to respond to the prevailing requirements of society and the institutions that derive support from it. These systems are not static as they are influenced by external, technological and many such developments. In this respect the educational

Many ideas in this paper were discussed in a paper entitled 'The Styles of Management Education in India' which was read at the International Conference on Management Education held at Xavier Institute of Management and Entrepreneurship, Bangalore, India.

system has to respond to these changes or it would lose its meaning and purpose. Among other requirements, the educational system has to contribute to the fund of knowledge-creation and that of societal and organisational processes. The present societal demands having changed in a significant manner, the educational system should respond differently to the emerging requirements of the situation. This is the perspective of the analysis in this book, not one of fault-finding. The approaches in the past were guided by the events and the circumstances at the time they were formulated and the present has to be guided by the situation as it now exists. Historical perspective is useful to understand the past but the present may not necessarily be an extension of the past. Hence, analysing the requirements of the present and relating one's action-choices to that is more meaningful than fault-finding with the past.

The strength of an educational institution, specially engaged in professional education, lies in expertise in many areas of knowledge and, at the same time integrating these areas in decision situations. A management programme, for example, relies heavily on theoretical bases of many academic disciplines such as economics, calculus and statistics, social science subjects, practice based areas such as engineering and technology. In management decision situations a practitioner has to understand the problem by analysing the influence of multiple factors in diagonising the situation. Even a teacher in economics would have to understand applications of his subject to develop a meaningful course for teaching in a professional school. This consideration does not mean that there is no room for pure theoretical explorations in a professional school but someone has to develop it in a way that it can become relevant for decision-making. Hence, each subject input has its own distinctive requirements and the leadership in a professional school has to recognise these and provide growth opportunity in each function. Simultaneously, the leader has to encourage openness and capability on the part of each function to integrate various subjects/areas.

The last 15 years have seen rapid growth of management schools in India. There are more than 1400 schools engaged in postgraduate level two-year educational programmes and every year, new institutions receive approval of All Indian Council of Technical Education (AICTE) which is a statutory body created in 1986 to regulate technical education in the country. The AICTE Act has given it vast powers to promote, develop, and regulate technical education in India. The Ministry has retained primarily the policy making function. The underlying purpose was that a professional body should promote and guide development of technical education in the country rather than the ministry of the government.

The concern for systematic growth of education and its quality standards by the government and the

AICTE are evident in the appointment of at least four committees during the last seven years for total review and recommendations by people engaged in, and concerned with, education. The Dayal Committee was appointed in January 2000 by the Ministry of Human Resource Development, Government of India to develop the Future Perspectives of Management Education. It had eighteen members who were vastly recognised and regarded in their respective fields such as management education, private and public sector business organisations, Planning Commission, University Grants Commission, AICTE and management consulting. The Committee gave its report to the government in April 2001.

The Ramaswamy P. Aiyar Committee was appointed in January 2003 by AICTE to Review Management Education. The Committee consisted of heads of highly respected and well-recognised management institutions, All India Management Association (AIMA), consulting organisations and AICTE. The U. R. Rao Committee was appointed by the Ministry of HRD, Government of India in 2002 to study the work of AICTE. The report was submitted to Government of India in September 2003. The S. L. Rao Committee was appointed by All India Management Association and submitted their report in 2005. There are many other committee reports available on specific issues such as accreditation, admission tests, common admission tests, and approach towards programmes of less than two-years duration. There have been many seminars and workshops to discuss the various reports arranged by professional bodies and teaching institutions. The major recommendations contained in reports are repeated as critical areas needing attention for enhancing quality of education by most people in these discussions (Dogra, 2005). These concerns broadly relate to non-availability of faculty, development of teaching material, inadequate attention to research, excessive control on curriculum and physical space requirements, faculty standards and many essential aspects of management programmes. The underlying assumption in the approach of the Regulatory bodies appears to suggest that standardisation of physical inputs, academic qualifications *per sé*, and centralised system of examination would improve the quality of education. However, none of these measures have upgraded the quality of education significantly, and I believe there is need to examine this assumption in the approach to promoting and controlling education.

The various committees were appointed by the HRD Ministry in Government of India, AICTE, and AIMA who are concerned with management education, suggests that they needed an overall review of education by knowledgeable people for initiating purposeful action to further improve the quality of education in the country. However, there is little evidence that the recommendations have led to any noticeable action. Most people engaged in management education feel that if another committee were to be appointed now in the year 2009, the same strengths and weaknesses are likely to be re-stated as brought out in earlier reports.

This review is based on the various reports of the committees, survey of 108 institutions, the available literature on the subject and my own personal experience.

The Current Status of Management Education and some Contemporary Issues

After independence in 1947, India was fortunate to have visionaries who recognised the importance of a strong democratic socio-political structure and saw urgent need for a many-sided economic, social and political development. For planned growth, the government set up an independent Planning Commission in March 1950 which could harness intellectual resources to develop national plans so that balanced growth could be achieved. Within this context a variety of institutions of scientific research, education, training and community development were initiated in the 50s.

Part-time courses for practicing executives were started in Kolkata University in 1953, followed by the universities of Delhi, Mumbai and Chennai. For training of senior executives, Administrative Staff College was set up in Hyderabad, National Institute of Industrial Engineering in Mumbai, National Productivity Council in Delhi, Indian Institute of Public Administration in Delhi, All India Management Association and many others (Chowdhary, 1999). All these institutions were started in the 1950s with collaboration and support from various known institutions abroad.

In 1959, the Government of India invited George W. Robbins, Associate Dean, Graduate School of Business Administration, University of California, Los Angeles to study and suggest how best management education of the requisite standard could be initiated and developed in India. The report of Dean Robbins recommended setting up an all-India based Institute of Management. The government decided to set up two Institutes of Management (IIMs), one in Kolkata in 1961 and another in Ahmedabad in 1962. These institutes were set up outside the domain of University Grants Commission and funded direct by the Ministry. The overall view was that the university system in India at that time was too rigid to be able to provide the flexibility and development processes that such an institution would require. The institute at Kolkata had collaboration arrangement with the Sloan School of Management, Massachusetts Institute of Technology (MIT), and Ahmedabad had a tie-up with Harvard Business School. Both IIMs started a two years M.B.A. level programme and short courses for practising executives in general management and functional areas. The nature of collaboration is important to briefly mention here because it is different from the practise found in many institutions in India over the last 15 years. The faculty members from the collaborating institutions came for long periods at a time. Most of the faculty stayed for 2-3 years and worked together with the faculty from India. The other significant feature of this collaboration was that MIT faculty, for example, did not impose their curriculum upon IIM, Kolkata. Rather, the local and the visiting faculty members worked together to develop what was relevant for the Indian situation. The programme evolved through genuine collaborative effort of all members of the faculty. Most of us had little experience of postgraduate level educational programmes for management. A majority of the faculty members of the Indian faculty came from business positions or with subject specialisation from university background. The method of developing the programme gave many of us confidence and overall perspective of what the courses in the programme should achieve. As a member of the faculty who had served in industry for around 15 years and came to a teaching position for the first time, I felt more confident in a new role. This approach gave most of us an integrative perspective of a management programme. Both the institutions developed a range of executive development programmes and close collaboration with industry.

The members of the local faculty and the foreign faculty were involved in designing, conducting and reviewing the programmes. They were also involved in consulting projects.

In the 60s many universities also set up full time postgraduate level programmes. Some of the universities had visiting faculty from abroad for varying periods and executives from industry who opted for an educational career. Many faculty members also went abroad for training or doctoral work.

The Early Approaches

Many management schools were started without adequate planning for financial, manpower and academic resources. Three types of inadequacies developed in the teaching of management programmes. These are briefly discussed below:

1. **Non-availability of faculty** : In early years the Institutes at Kolkata and Ahmedabad recruited faculty from universities in the USA and the UK Indians who were completing their doctoral studies in American universities, or in other countries abroad were interviewed and suitable candidates were offered jobs on the spot. Similar search for suitable faculty was aggressively made in India from the university and business community. The institutes also started doctoral level courses to meet faculty requirements. But the growth was faster than

the numbers of persons available with requisite background. Hence all teaching institutions experienced shortage in respect to their manpower requirement. As the gap between salary levels of teachers in the universities in USA and India became wider, fewer Indians opted to come back to India and many opted to settle down in foreign countries. Foreign universities offered opportunities to graduates in their own country as they were also expanding and needed people with requisite background. As such, this source of attracting qualified individuals shrunk to a large extent.

2. **Inadequate concern for developing indigenous teaching material :** The second difficulty that arose from the situation prevailing in India, barring the Institutes of Management and a few urban-based universities, was that the faculty used teaching methodology that was most familiar to them in their own university programmes. Apart from this, the faculty had limited opportunity to interact with industry in terms of executive teaching programmes or research. Hence much of the teaching became somewhat similar to teaching of subject-based courses in a university department. Thus, management educational programmes stood at two levels during the period of 60s and 70s: one, institutions where the faculty had opportunity to travel, do research, had freedom to pursue industry

or client-specific activity and many of them became known and accepted both in academic and industry environment. They could innovate and contribute papers in journals abroad and in many cases teach for varying periods in courses abroad. At another level, the institutions offered limited opportunity to develop perspectives of a professional programme of study with limited scope to test their ideas in live business situations. The teaching became highly textbook oriented.

With the growth of institutions in India in the 70s, 80s and the 90s, the problems that the institutions experienced in terms of their manpower requirements, access to industry and meaningful interaction between the faculty and industry, etc. became more acute than before. The differences that characterised the two types of institutions continued and a larger number came closer to the second type. This concern is expressed in the various reports on management education mentioned earlier. These reports have also suggested remedial action but response to all such matters is still awaited.

3. **Lack of concern for relevance of the content of courses :** A third problem of considerable importance concerns the direction of management education in the country. Inadequate attention to research and organisational studies have resulted in

a predominantly Western bias in educational programmes without even testing the validity of what was taught from the available books. Kamla Chowdhry, who was intimately involved in early years in 1960s with Indian Institute of Management in Ahemdabad, wrote in 1988.

> "If management education in India is to have an identity of its own, it must have its own views and ways of thinking about progress, development, responsibility, authority, commitment etc. Management education to be effective should not be merely an adoption of techniques of cost benefit analysis, marketing strategies, O.B. etc. but reflect the values and priorities of the country. Although the first steps were taken by early institution builders of management education in the country to integrate it to the priorities of the country, this process has not advanced sufficiently, nor with much effectiveness...."

Further, Chowdhry added:

> "Management Education in India, along with other higher education, has built an edifice of learning but has been deprived of its foundations- foundations rooted in the social, economic, political and cultural life of the people" (Philip and Shankar Narayan, 1989, p.3).

Similar concerns were raised by the National Policy on education in 1986 and the work done by the research based reports of Dayal (1998); D. P. Sinha (2004) and others. A serious enquiry into the impact of socio-cultural ethos of India was not possible given the circumstances leading to growth of management institutions in India. This situation prevails except that some individuals in this area have incorporated such issues in their writings and teaching (Sinha 2004; Chakraborty 1987; Dayal, 1977; Kakar 1971).

In broad terms the management schools can be categorised at three levels, as follows:

Category I : Institutions which have mechanisms built into the system for self-renewal and compare very favourably with the internationally recognised institutions. This category would have around 30-40 institutions.

Category II : Institutions with adequate resources which are struggling to upgrade their standards. This category will roughly have around 30-35 per cent of the institutions.

Category III : Institutions which have extremely limited financial and faculty resources to satisfactorily align their programmes with developments in the market. Most such institutions are sponsored and controlled by individuals primarily to promote their business interests. They seem to conduct their programmes in a routine mould. This category has the largest number among the existing institutions.

The three categories are based on a survey carried out by the Dayal Committee, personal visits to a large number of institutions, information available on the website of the institutions and discussion with Directors and Faculty members in formal and informal meetings. The categorisation and percentages are estimates and not based on systematic analysis of data. However, many other knowledgeable people in education broadly agree with the break up suggested here.

My discussion below relates primarily to category II and III institutions because category I institutions are mainly self-driven and alive to the changing environment. They have evolved mechanisms to review and upgrade their activities at regular intervals as the highly rated institutions abroad do. Another strong point of these institutions is that they have strict entrance requirements based exclusively on the performance of a student. Some of these institutions have developed material that concern the society in the East. For example, extremely meaningful inputs are available in spiritualism (Chakraborty 1987; Siddiqui 2005), communication in rural community, consumer behaviour, rural marketing, cross-cultural issues and diversity. In many cases centres for intensive research and training have been created within the framework of the institutions. The literature on change management is rich and relevant for our societies. A large number of businesses in India are family managed. Many such businesses have led industrial growth in the past but seem to be loosing their primacy in the last few years. A great deal of literature on family dynamics and business demands has become available. (Dayal et. al., 2007; Jain, 2006). Some institutions have a separate package of courses for family businesses. The continuing contact of faculty with industry and consulting gives opportunity in this category of institutions to undertake study in new areas of relevance to industry.

The Academic Status of Category II and III Institutions

Invariably, institutions in category II and a substantial number in category III follow the practices and procedures that category I employ but the process—the way these tasks are carried out—lack rigour and conviction. There are variations from one institution to another, but the commonly observed patterns identified in various reports are mentioned below:

1. Admission, grading, class attendance and student discipline are included in the manuals of the concerned institutions but many of these aspects are often compromised in action.
2. Faculty involvement in course planning is minimal. Invariably, outlines are obtained from available sources and used. The package of courses is usually weak and not well-integrated.

3. Teaching methodology commonly used consists of lectures. Examination patterns are also designed to test knowledge, not application. The courses have somewhat limited focus on developing capabilities in problem-solving, data analysis, diagnosis and decision-making. There is little concern for individual growth and development.
4. Each course is seen as a separate and stand alone subject of study. There is little effort to have interactions among faculty in academic content of the courses. In one institution a faculty member of long standing mentioned that the outlines are available if anyone wants to see them. Another faculty member said, in response, how does anyone know whether the outline represents what is taught in class. Many institutions did not have written down course outlines.
5. Institutional management in most institutions neither encourage research nor give credit to a faculty member if individual initiative is taken by someone. Even the research undertaken appear to have limited applicability for operating organisations (Bennis & O' Toole, 2005).
6. Most institutions do not have contact with industry and business except in respect to placement of students for jobs. In some cases practicing managers are invited for occasional lectures.

7. Very few institutions organise short courses for practising executives or maintain work-level contact with industry.

Sectoral Programmes

With growth in economy, different sectors have come up and the management has initiated training and education for sector-specific courses. Agriculture received early attention and therefore many institutions exist in this sector. Forestry is another area. Programmes in hotel management, retail business, tourism, plantation have been primarily initiated by the industry for their own network with few exceptions. The need for sector specific courses and educational facilities have yet to catch up with the demand. I believe that sector-specific courses would require partnership between industry and educational institutions. They would also need flexibility which the Indian educational system will have to develop. In these courses there is a strong component of general and functional management interwoven with particular task features of the sector. Academic institutions by themselves cannot initiate knowledge of the nitty gritty of the sector. The strength of sector-specific courses would lie in collaboration.

Some Concerns for Institutional Development

There are two kinds of inputs that need special attention—factors from external agencies that influence internal functioning of the institution (Dayal, 1967), and internal issues that facilitate or hinder creativity.

External Factors

The institutions engaged in management education come under the jurisdiction of the University Grants Commission (UGC) or All India Council of Technical Education (AICTE). In order to ensure subject coverage and the quality of the programme, the UGC prescribes a curriculum and minimum teaching material for each course. The quality is measured in terms of centrally prepared examination and grading by the university concerned. A certain percentage is assigned for internal evaluation. Hence, standardisation of courses, teaching material and evaluation is considered necessary to maintain the quality of education. The underlying assumption in this practice appears to be that a curriculum prepared by an expert body, and followed by institutions, would ensure quality standards of education. Examination based on the curriculum would further ensure that the institutions follow the outline.

In broad terms, AICTE shares the same belief in their approach to the regulatory function. They prescribe what is a desirable structure, content of a programme, by whom it should be conducted, and the system of grading, staff, physical space, etc. The functioning of an institution is reviewed against these norms or standards and deviation from these invites disqualification. The same approach is reflected in the accreditation procedure.

In 1960, when the report of Dean Robbins was being discussed by the government which resulted in setting up of Indian Institutes of Management the point was strongly made that management education needs flexibility, innovation and close linkages with industry which rigidity in university system would not provide. The requirements of management education are still valid and the institutions engaged in management education must deeply be concerned about innovation in their programmes, teaching methodology, external linkages, etc. It would appear that the UGC/AICTE approaches have extended their control mechanism from discipline-based programmes without adequate attention given to requirements of professional programmes.

The table below shows approaches to the regulatory systems in India and the West in some key areas.

Approaches to the Regulatory Systems in India and the West

	Indian Approach	Western Approach
1. Who regulates	AICTE, UGC	Professional bodies on voluntary basis + Market mechanism
2. Course coverage	Prescribed–outline, classroom hours, etc.	Determined by the institution concerned
3. Quality of the programme	Prescribe–no. of teachers, qualifications, examination, grading, etc.	Market/student acceptance – open system

Cont.

4. Compliance	Standards laid down for course work; faculty; physical and support systems–non-compliance invites punitive action	No predetermined standards
5. Accreditation	- Compulsory by law - Inspection team sent by AICTE reports on adherence to pre-determined standards–failure to keep to them invites disqualification	Voluntary professional Association based on the vision, goals, plans of the institution - seen as internal audit - visiting team is trained - total freedom–develop institutional expertise/ uniqueness
6. Underlying assumption	Standards laid down by expert bodies would ensure coverage and quality of the programme.	Constant review by internal teams.

Educational institutions in the West operate at two levels (i) they believe that market is the best judge of quality and institutions that fall below market expectations would have to improve or, without support of industry, cease to function, (ii) the coverage of the academic programme and the approach of the educational institution is influenced by reports of professional bodies. Such bodies also undertake accreditation of the institution on request to ensure that it provides aspects that facilitate academic programmes and have processes that determine quality of inputs. Basically, the institutional management analyses in depth the internal processes and prepares an analytical report. This report forms the basis for review of the work of the institution by the accreditation team which is appointed by a professional body. Members who visit for purposes of accreditation have to undergo training for the purpose. They are concerned with the process, *i.e.* how things are done, besides what the institution does. This process is seen as an audit exercise for the benefit of the institution concerned. The team is able to provide help to the institution to re-look those aspects which need improvement. The accreditation has value for the concerned institution in the market because of the thoroughness by recognised professionals who undertake the task.

The institutions do have a framework for the programmes but there is considerable flexibility to develop their academic activities. I believe that flexibility has contributed to innovation and creativity in the better known institutions such as Harvard, Wharton, Columbia, Stanford and others.

Besides broad guidelines for institutional programmes, the Western regulatory system is open. The quality of output is determined by the usefulness and relevance by the user-bodies such as business organisations. The institution has to be in touch with the markets and review its processes and activities to link them with changes taking place around it. The institution has to undertake a variety of activities such as executive development programmes, research, publication, consulting, etc. by which the user-bodies can assess its quality. Institutions cannot afford to function in isolation as many such institutions do in India.

What Price Indian Approach

Standardisation encourages, more often than not, mediocrity (Merton, 1957; Dayal, 1967). It provides comfort to individuals to operate within the confines of the box. Teachers are tempted to pick up previous years outline and fill up the blanks. They do not have to question the relevance of the material, design of the course, the methodology, or market developments. Some enthusiastic individuals may add some material here and there but they can carry on the job without doing so.

Research in innovation (Lester and Piore, 2004; Bernstein, 1988; Dayal, 1991) suggests that new approaches, new thinking and breakthroughs inevitably require interaction within and outside the confines of the organisation. In institutions such as the Indian Institutes of Management where I have served as a teacher and later as chief executive, the teachers had to prepare their own outlines of courses and present those to other faculty for open discussion and questioning. On one occasion, for example, while presenting a course outline, the faculty pointed out why I have not looked for more recent cases rather than continue to use the ones that were written years ago. This led to renewed search and serious examination of the course package. In another presentation of a course by a faculty, a question was raised as to how the objectives of the course would be met by the methodology employed by the instructor. At IIM, Ahmedabad the faculty appraisal system, considered among other things, the quality of material developed and new material brought into the course. We were able to bring into class teaching the findings of our research and insights gained in consulting projects. Such inputs were appreciated by students in their rating of teachers in the institute bulletin.

The negative consequences of the regulatory approaches in India have been that faculty has felt no need to look outside the confines of institutions, or think seriously about the relevance of what and how they teach, or even develop themselves to their individual potential (Dayal, 2008). The market mechanism does not seem to be strong enough to influence changes as it is in countries abroad. This situation may arise as business organisations become more discriminating on account of competition. It wouldn't be surprising if AICTE would also have to do some critical appraisal of its approach to regulation.

The regulatory systems developed by UGC/AICTE exercise control of institutions and compliance to some norms set up by them. Total energies of these organisations are directed toward ensuring how closely the institutions comply to the norms. In contrast management controls systems in highly productive organisations in India are designed to look inwards by the organisation concerned, and not as threats for reprisal. Most international studies have brought out that Indians have strong predilection for personal power and authority, and it is likely that this factor contributes to devising controls by regulatory bodies.

Internal Factor : The Leadership

The task system of education is different from that of a business organisation. A. K. Rice who had reviewed IIM, Ahmedabad in early 70s, made the point that the Institute had sixty systems (there were sixty members of the faculty at that time) and each one is different from the others. As mentioned earlier, an academic institution needs individual contribution and each person needs workspace and a supporting environment to do so. Simultaneously, the institution needs a collective institutional mechanism and a culture of working together. The institutional leadership has to sensitively develop systems and practices where both these conditions can prevail. An academic institution cannot obtain the requisite environment unless it is able to develop what Barnard has called spontaneous will to cooperate. The system needs, among its people, diversity to generate and experiment with ideas. In the situations where I have spent my academic life, differences, heated arguments, open critiquing and seemingly irreconcilable issues were often experienced in meetings and I personally believe that such events led to developing cohesiveness, respect for others and tolerance, provided that leadership handled such situations wisely. The manner in which the leader handle such situations establishes his authority and influence. At the same time there are matters which institutional leader has to handle notwithstanding the opposition to the issue in hand. The faculty at IIM, Ahmedabad was not in favour of the agriculture programme but the director went ahead with the plans that he had in mind. I can recall a few instances in IIM, Lucknow when, as Director, I went ahead with certain programmes after explaining the reasons for doing so.

Authority and power are complex issues in an educational institution. In a large measure the leader is able to acquire influence (power) in the system when he is able to develop among the members what has been called limits of freedom to act. Brown has called it discretionary element of the job. This authority is derived from open debate and involvement of the community in decision-making. This situation arises when the system values consensus in decision-making on issues that concern the work community. My personal experience has repeatedly confirmed that peer-based social environment, rather than hierarchical authority pattern, generates creativity and a sense of personal responsibility at each level. In our study of 40 business schools in the year 2000 we found that the more respected institutions did function closer to the manner mentioned here.

Most educational institutions have authority centralised at higher echelons of administration. The authority flows top downward. The hierarchy is valued. Consultation is selective and often confined to a select group of loyal persons. In such an environment innovation and creativity as institutional characteristic are unlikely to flourish. The educational system in India has not been able to develop educational or training programmes to develop leadership capabilities for academic institutions. Some individuals have developed their own capabilities and belief systems to perform creditably in institutional roles. There has been discussion on this issue but as yet there is no formal system to provide systematic training for educational leadership. Most highly rated institutions have been able to depart from administrative practices that inhibit creativity and growth. They are able to attract individuals who have independence of thought, a strong belief system, patience and dedication to develop viable creative systems.

Lessons from the History of Development

I believe that the history of development of management education has many lessons. Perhaps it was necessary to set up legally autonomous institutions when IIMs were promoted in 60s. This pattern has continued over the years. I believe that it was necessary at the start itself to strengthen the university departments. Dayal Committee has suggested in their Report that the university system has a distinct advantage for providing quality education because the management schools located within the university system can derive support from other departments to bring inter-subject inputs into the courses. The university is best placed to take up research in the many areas of management, provided they are able to change the structures and the processes which can make them more creative and responsive to developments in society. Even the newer universities set up in the last 20 years or so have followed the model of older universities. The only noticeable contribution some of the newer universities have made is that they have been able to introduce departments and centres with interdisciplinary focus, and start a few job-oriented courses. Some of the longer established universities have also done this. The individual contributions to knowledge have come in spite of the system. They have failed to design the kind of flexibility in the educational system as the universities abroad are able to provide especially in the United States. I believe that what a strong university department can do in terms of inter-functional knowledge, interdisciplinary research and publications, few independent institutions can undertake. Such institutions have commercial limitations to provide library, technology, research, publications, etc. because most such activities require heavy financial expenditure without commensurate returns in terms of funds. They create knowledge but do not give immediate financial returns. However, some of the independent institutions have been able to undertake applied research but they are invariably supported by trusts or corporate bodies.

The university departments of management study need greater autonomy, flexibility in operations, and systems that can trigger growth. By creating a large number of autonomous institutions with relatively higher income opportunities and better working environment, the manpower is diverted away from the universities, depriving them of resources to take up knowledge-addition tasks.

In brief, the affordable and—high quality education—teaching, research, knowledge development etc.– is more likely to become available through university system rather than the network of autonomous institutions, provided they are encouraged to reorient themselves and given requisite levels of operational and financial freedom. Any effort to regulate fee structure in autonomous institutions to make education affordable is likely to be dysfunctional. Reduction in revenues will cut out knowledge generation activities such as research, case writing, publication, etc. rendering most institutions to be engaged mainly in teaching from textbooks. There is need for certain number of independent institutions which are able to obtain continuing corporate support or those managed by substantial trusts. With stable sources of resources and opportunities such institutions could experiment with new ideas and contribute towards knowledge creation.

References

The Reports Mentioned in the Paper

Dayal, I '*Report and Recommendations of the Committee on Policy-Perspectives for Management Education*', Ministry of Human Resource Development, Government of India, New Delhi, April, 2001.

Ramaswamy P Aiyar Committee on '*Management Education Review*', All India Council for Technical Education, New Delhi, 2003.

S L Rao Committee on '*Management Education in India*', All India Management Association, New Delhi, 2004-2005.

U R Rao Committee on the '*Review of the AICTE and Suggest Steps for Improvement*', Ministry of HRD, Govt. of India, New Delhi, September, 2003.

Some Issue-based Committees

Government of India appointed committee on rationalisation of admission tests, July, 2003.

AICTE appointed committees

(a) D. V. Singh Committee on Common Entrance Tests, May, 1999.

(b) Abad Ahmed Committee to Review Accreditation Format, 2005.

(c) Ishwar Dayal Committee to recommend on AICTE role for courses with less than 2 years duration.

Books and Articles

1. Bennis, W G and O'Toole, J, *How Business Schools Lost Their Way*, Harvard Business Review, May, 2005.
2. Bernstein, J (1988). *Three Degrees Above Zero*, Affiliated East-West Press, New Delhi.
3. Chakraborty, S K (1987). *Managerial Effectiveness and Quality of Work Life*, Tata McGraw-Hill, New Delhi.
4. Chowdhary, S (1999). *Management Education in India,* Institute of Management Technology, Ghaziabad.
5. Dayal, I, et. al., (2007). *Family Management, Multinational and Public Sector Enterprises*, Ane Books India, New Delhi.
6. Dayal, I (2008). *Teaching of Management*, Ane Books India, New Delhi.

7. Dayal, I (1998). *Reappraising Management Education, Perspectives for Future,* Mittal Publications, New Delhi.

8. Dayal, I (1991). *Managing Innovation*, Concept Publishing Co., New Delhi.

9. Dayal, I (1977). *Change in Work Organisation*, Concept, New Delhi.

10. Dayal, I '*Constraints of Legislation on Organisational Effectiveness*', Indian Journal of Ind. Rel., New Delhi, 1967. Vol. 2, No. 3, pp. 315-332.

11. Dogra, D (Ed.) (2005). *Management Education—Issues and Predilections,* Excel Books, New Delhi.

12. Jain, R (2006). *Chains that Liberate-Governance of Family Firms,* Macmillan, New Delhi.

13. Kakar, S *Authority Patterns and Subordinate Behaviour in Indian Organisations in* Understanding Organisational Behaviour by Kamla Chowdhary and Sudhir Kakar, Tata McGraw-Hill, New Delhi, 1971 pp. 481-497.

14. Lester, R K and Piore, K J (2004). *Innovation, The Missing Link,* Harvard University Press, Cambridge, Massachusetts.

15. Merton, R K (1957). *Bureaucratic Structure and Personality* in Social Theory, Social Structure, Free Press of Glencoe, New York.

16. Philip, J and Shankar Narayan, D (Ed.) (1989). *Management Education in India*, IIM, Bangalore, Bangalore.

17. Siddiqui, M (2005). *Corporate Soul, The Monk within the Manager*, Response Books, New Delhi.

18. Sinha, D P (2004). *Management Education in India, Perspectives and Challenges,* The ICFAI University Press, Hyderabad.

6

A Perspective of Professional Education

Every few years one comes across a spade of articles in newspapers, and listens to discussions in public forums, that management programmes are not particularly useful. It is suggested that business orgnaisations have to groom individuals from business schools to equip them to handle managerial roles. Some articles on the subject have suggested that it is better to select bright students from a university department and train them in the company. Another repeatedly mentioned view is that practising managers should be engaged in teaching in management programmes in preference to persons drawn from academic streams.

I have no doubt that these comments are made by individuals who have come to these conclusions as a

---

Based on a paper read on this subject at an International Conference in Institute of Management Technology Ghaziabad in 2007.

result of their own and corporate experiences. As such, we have to respect them. I have no wish to comment on these views except that we need to be clear about what can be expected from the educational programmes, and what they cannot do.

The formal programmes of education for management began in 1898 in Philadelphia in the United States. From the early beginning, the programmes have undergone many changes based on formal reports on the subject and experiences of institutional leaders. Most countries throughout the world, including India, have, in a large measure, adopted the purpose, content and broad format, including the literature in various areas of study from the United States. Hence, it would be useful to briefly review developments in respect to purpose and course content during different phases of the programme in USA Management programmes were initiated by various departments such as economics, accounting, political economy, etc. in different universities. The orientation of management courses varied from one university to another. Chicago University developed a set of courses on subjects related to business. New York University had focus on accounting. In some schools like Wharton at the University of Pennsylvania the curricula included courses on government service, history, economics, accounting and business law. Harvard Business School was established under the college of arts and science in

1908 with a focus on general subjects. Wharton, Chicago and Harvard and other schools which placed more emphasis on practical business skills were more popular with organisations than those which followed a more theoretical approach. In substance, courses in different universities did not reflect any clear purpose or direction in their programmes.

In 1916, the American Association of Collegiate Schools of Business (AACSB) was set up by the business schools for development of management education. In 1926, AACSB laid down standards for business schools for admission to the Association. It held that business schools should offer reasonable amount of work in five areas–business finance, accounting, business law, marketing and statistics.

Each university developed its own package of courses and brought about changes and developments on their own in many areas, including methods of teaching the course. However, decisive changes in management education resulted from two landmark reports in late 1950s—Pierson report by a committee set up by Carnegie Foundation and Gordon and Howell report by a committee set up by Ford Foundation. The reports were concerned about the intellectual quality of students entering business schools and advocated higher standards of admission and stricter performance standards in MBA programmes. They advocated that courses should develop capability among students to apply scientific methods and provide general societal knowledge to business policy issues. The course should provide broad education rather than specialists in certain business areas.

The Gordon and Howell report specifically suggested that business education required classification of its objectives and direction. They suggested that business education should prepare students for careers in business. They felt that programmes in various schools were too diverse, and suggested a broad curriculum for MBA level programmes. They observed that there was excessive specialisation in the programmes of many schools. Such specialisation does not fulfill the purpose of the business.

In more recent times the Porter and Mckibin Committee report in the 1980s has emphasised that MBA level course should generate vision, and not problem solving skills alone. They also suggested that there is need to better integrate the functional areas.

Individual business schools such as those at Harvard, Sloan School at MIT, Stanford, and Columbia and others set up their own committees from time to time to review their programmes to align them with requirements of their markets. Summarising the significant developments brought about in management education in the USA over time, the following considerations need special mention for our purpose.

1. The business programme at MBA level should be designed to prepare managers in all relevant areas of concern, not specialists.
2. The content of these programmes should have both theoretical and practical components in areas of its concern. Furthermore, the courses should provide vision, a futuristic perspective, and not merely problem-diagnostic and problem-resolution capabilities among students.
3. The institutions should be engaged in aligning their programmes to changes in the business environment and business practices.
4. The programme at MBA level should be concerned with practical application of what is taught and develop managerial capabilities.
5. The emphasis and content of the educational programme should change to respond to market and business situations.

The Nature of the Programme

We need to distinguish between education and training. Educational programmes provide a wide range of knowledge, which can help a person understand the environment in which he functions and acquires systematic knowledge to understand why things happen as they do and ways of resolving problem areas. They help individuals to relate better to immediate issues and problems in the wider context of a given situation. After attending an educational programme it is expected that an individual is better able to understand the totality and cope with it in effective ways, and provide better direction to deal with the situation by virtue of the knowledge, awareness and association with others. An individual should acquire a professional approach, capability to deal with organisational and social issues and problems by applying knowledge gained in a programme of study, and become a responsive citizen. Not all individuals may acquire these in the same measure, but the educational process is meant to channelise individuals in this direction, depending upon the predilections of the concerned person.

Education has to develop an individuals' competence in many ways. It develops capability among individuals to differentiate between what is objective and what is subjective, sharpens sensitivity to people and situations, and helps individuals to carve out a responsible role in society. Whether all educational programmes fully, or partially, serve this purpose or not, the programme objective and supporting package to achieve the purpose is necessary. All aspects of the institution that contribute to the set goal need to develop in harmony. It must include the curriculum, the teaching methodology, the teaching faculty, the administrative systems, and the institutional leadership. They should collectively provide the necessary conditions to serve the purpose. Perhaps only a few institutions serve the function effectively but these conditions are necessary to achieve the purpose for which the institutions are set up.

Training is more specific. It has a defined goal, and an identifiable outcome. In a professional programme of study some elements, to a limited extent, may be common to both education and training but the focus of each is different.

There is much concern for limited number of career-oriented courses in universities. This is indeed a valid concern. University education should enable graduates to have an occupation. Job-orientation has to be, however, considered in a wider context of the emerging socio-economic developments in the country. MBA is designed to develop an overall managerial capability, not a specific skill.

Career Related Courses

In the West individuals with qualifications in social and hard sciences obtain satisfying positions in areas where knowledge acquired in the university courses is useful. In most cases the subject knowledge is necessary for a wide range of professional careers. As our economy and social system institutions develop, we would need individuals with background in many subjects. In a limited way this is already happening. The university programmes, however, would have to be re-oriented to develop applied focus in teaching. Universities are in a better position to provide career orientation in those areas which benefit by understanding the theoretical and conceptual bases. Primarily, skill-based courses are more competently handled by a polytechnic or skill-oriented institution.

The University Structure

The university system in India is highly structured into art or science or technology, etc. streams. These requirements may have been relevant at the time the system was devised, and choice of professions was extremely limited, but it totally fails to serve the requirements of the current situation. If the educational system has to provide opportunities to serve the purpose as stated earlier, individuals would have to have much greater scope for choice of subjects and courses. For example, a student who may be registered for a degree in whatever area of study should have scope to take courses in other subjects to widen his perspective. A student must have scope to experiment and choose a vocation based on a realistic assessment of his/her own interests. Students would take studies more seriously if a subject is chosen according to their own needs or interest as against a situation where they are obliged to take a course on someone else's suggestion. The lack of personal involvement in learning also results from limited choices provided by the educational system, as now.

Because our university system is unable to provide the flexibility needed in the emerging environment, we have created independent institutions to handle career-related areas. I believe that this is a poor substitute to developing the university system. Specialised institutions concentrate primarily on the specific task-related subjects; they are unable to offer a wider choice of subjects to students. Apart from weakening the university system, this approach inadequately serves the requirements of education *viz.* greater awareness of the society around an individual and definition of one's own role in society.

Professional Education

The professional education in management has added responsibilities. Broadly stated, these are following:

- Besides a wider range in socio-political and economic areas the programme has to provide knowledge-base relevant for undertaking managerial responsibility
- Develop, through interventions in teaching pedagogy or course structure, confidence to use knowledge to effectively deal with organisation and task-related situations
- Develop capabilities in respect to behavioural, attitude and value that are required in managerial roles
- Imbibe the code of conduct and the obligations of the profession including responsibility to wider society.

These requirements must become the core of the educational programme in management. Professional programmes have to extend beyond teaching courses in the classroom. They have to develop personal capabilities of individuals in terms of values and societal obligations. The most important among these are sensitivity towards people, ability to influence people, adaptability to work in groups, develop self-awareness, a value frame, etc. The ability to use knowledge in dealing with organisational and business situations requires hands-on experience. Other professional programmes such as medicine, chartered accountancy, architecture, law and others are able to provide either live or simulated situations to support classroom learning. Some management programmes also include simulation experiences such as business games, role-play, and scenario building exercises etc. These are very useful but cover only a specific aspect of management.

In the West business organisations have opened their doors to management schools to offer real life experiences to students. At the London School of Business, for example, students are engaged in consulting projects in industry as part of their regular MBA course. In some schools in the USA students spend afternoon hours in doing work in companies. R. W. Revans in Belgium developed action-learning methodology for education of managers. The participants were engaged in specific tasks assigned by participating organisations, and the progress was discussed in weekly classroom sessions which were attended by all participants and the faculty.

In the review meetings the individual concerned was able to gain insights about his work and related areas. Most programmes have to provide experience to handle problems and learn from the exercise. Management institutions in the West have succeeded in obtaining cooperation of business organisations in organising live experiences for students. In India except the Indian Business School in Hyderabad, such relationships between educational institutions and business organisations has yet to develop. The 6-8 week summer placement of students in business organisations is a poor substitute to the experience that is available in the West.

Harvard Business School devised the case-method of teaching in the mid 30s for their postgraduate courses. This was a kind of device to bring a real-life decision problem from the business organisation for students to work on. It was also a way of bringing the business organisation to the classroom. The teachers wrote up a decision situation as the manager faced it at the time it occurred. The case writer interviewed individuals who were involved in the situation and, where necessary, provided the relevant details of the company and its environment. This case posed a live dynamic situation for students to identify the problem, analyse data, diagnose what had led to the problem, and decide on its resolution after examining the possible consequences of each of the possible solutions.

In a typical two-year programme of study, a student is required to analyse somewhere around 500 odd cases. The cases familiarise a student with the environment of business and the organisational dynamics, apart from developing his analytical capabilities. The case-teacher provides reading materials that familiarise the student with research findings, concepts and theories in the area of concern. During the discussion in class, a student is able to evaluate his analysis and diagnosis of the problem with that of the other students and recognise his own strengths and weaknesses or biases in analysing a situation. The case discussion in class provides students with the opportunity to learn to influence others and also become sensitive to the views of others. A class composed of students with varied backgrounds is a near prototype of a typical company and this prepares a student to handle situations in his future role. As we know, the case-method of teaching is based on the premise that individuals learn by working on problems and sharing ideas with peers. To the best of my knowledge, except the Indian Institute of management at Ahmedabad, no other institute in India follows the case-method of teaching. I believe that even at IIM-A the rigour of this method has now been diluted from its early days in the 60s and the 70s. Case method of teaching, and not casual use of cases as commonly done in many schools in India, serves more than any other known method the requirements of management education as identified earlier (Dayal, 2008).

The case-method is not without its shortcomings. The student never knows whether his solution solves the problem in hand, or not. He arrives at a solution without knowing the difficulties in implementing the solution of the problem arrived at in class. Some students are left with a feeling of incompleteness. In the Indian situation, where students come to a management programme without any work experience, the reality of the work life and the socio-political processes in an organisation are not fully appreciated, and there is a fair chance that solutions ignore the complexity of organisational dynamics.

Another criticism is that having done 500 odd cases a person is inclined to seek solutions of problems at work that applied to similar problems in class discussion, without looking at it as a fresh problem with its own multiple dimensions. Personally, I have not found these shortcomings to be serious. However, a case teacher is well-advised to keep such considerations in mind. I believe that advantages of the case-method of teaching far outweigh the disadvantages.

In brief, management education improves students' capabilities to adjust to an organisation and assume managerial responsibility in the shortest time possible. The programme specifically prepares a student in respect to the following:

1. A student imbibes the scientific approach to systematically deal with business and organisational problems. The study of management prepares him to seek causal relationships and attempts to deal with factors that induce a problem rather than the symptom. The body of knowledge from readings and interactions with others in a two-year long programme cultivates these perspectives.
2. The programme develops interpersonal skills and ability to deal with people at work. These capabilities develop slowly in orgnisations, and sometimes do not develop at all among individuals without such training.
3. The programme familiarises an individual with the socio-political and economic environment of business, and to a large extent, the organisational dynamics. The assignments, cases, interaction with visiting faculty, reading material and project work better prepare a student to deal with issues and problems in the global context. In organisations these perspectives develop over a long period of time.
4. To a large extent, in a well-designed programme of study, a student begins to crystallise his values and

citizen-role and responsibility, and develops a degree of self-reliance.

5. Students are able to cope with critical organisational processes such as diversity, consensus-building and many other demands in life after closely working with a large number of students and faculty who come from many different backgrounds and orientations.

6. An educational programme does not train a person for a job or a specific position; it prepares an individual for a career. A concentration package in elective courses may equip a person with somewhat deeper knowledge in a given area but a job requires more than subject knowledge. A job, I believe, can only be learnt when a person is engaged in dealing with problems in the context of an operating system. Educational background helps him to pursue the organisation tasks in a systematic and analytical way.

Mr. R. Gopal Krishnan, Vice President of Tata Sons, and earlier, with Hindustan Unilever, in his recent book has said that a manager has to continuously learn many things from his work—from his failures, from observation, from his colleagues and supervisors–because his capacity to handle an increasing level of responsibility will depend on his learning new things. He points out that management education provides a strong foundation but successful managers have to learn from doing things on their own, keep up with new knowledge by reading, attending programmes and assimilating knowledge.

We have to recognise that even the best educational programmes cannot teach everything that a manager has to do. This is so because some things can only be learnt on the job within the context of a company. Education disciplines thinking and encourages a maturer outlook on life in the job he is given to do. An employer has to build on acquired knowledge and competence, those aspects of the managerial role that can only be learnt by engaging in work. We have to develop closer collaboration between the management institutions and business organisations. This will benefit both.

We need to also recognise that theories and concepts in the classroom must have applied orientation irrespective of the background of the teacher. If a practicing manager teaches a course, he must have adequate level of familiarity with research findings on the subject, and also the literature. He must be able to evaluate his experience in the context of authentic data from a number of organisations as the researcher does. If the course is taught by a person coming from an academic stream, he must test the theories and concepts in real-life situations from research and consulting, or in any other way. Collaboration between educational institutions and industry has to go way beyond teaching in class.

As in business, or any other institutional activity, some management schools are good and some others are lacking in many areas. This is true in India as in other countries. Whatever the market standing of an institution, it is important that the perspective of education is clear and we strive to improve areas in which we in management education can contribute the most.

References

Dayal, I (2008). *Teaching of Management*, Ane Books India, New Delhi.

Gopal Krishna, R (2007). *Case of Bonsai Manager, Lessons from Nature of Growing*, Penguin Books, New Delhi.

Gordon, R A and Howell, J E (1959). *Higher Education in Business*, Columbia University Press, New York.

Pierson, F C (1959). *The Education of American Business*, McGraw-Hill, New York.

Porter L W and Mckibbin, L E (1988). *Management Education and Development: Drift or Thrust into the 21st Century,* McGraw-Hill, New York.

7

Impact of Wider Culture on Organisational Effectiveness

Effective Organisations

The emerging competitive environment of business has posed new challenges for organisations and public service institutions. They face more challenges in three respects:

- The need to develop an environment of creativity and innovation which has given a competitive edge to fast developing organisations in the West, Japan and Korea
- The need to generate ways for mental preparedness of managers and employees to seek and develop technology

---

Many ideals in this chapter appeared in a paper on the subject in Indian J. of I.R., Vol. 43 No. 1 pp. 87-99

- The need to develop mental willingness at the top and senior levels of management in a large number of established organisations to bring about changes in their styles of managing (Dayal, et. al., 2007).

Some organisations have grown through either entrepreneurial decision to acquire assets, or collaboration arrangements through which they have obtained access to technology, and in a few rare cases developed new products though their existing development departments. As brought out in Chapter 4, the process of innovation, and the managerial support needed to sustain it, are different from the centralised control and hierarchical styles prevailing in the Indian situation.

Our studies also suggest that copying the successful models of management in the West do not guarantee success in the Indian context. This chapter poses some basic issues in reorienting our management perspectives. The earlier chapters in this book have highlighted the need for reorienting our educational system. Organisational imperatives in this chapter shows the need for intensive research by the university academic community and experimental approaches to help organisations to prepare for new challenges in the competitive situation. This is the scenario that the academic community and the organisational leadership should share.

Success of organisations in a competitive situation relies largely on achieving cost-effectiveness, quality of product, product innovation, ability to anticipate and quickly adapt to the emerging market demands, creativity and innovation. Most organisations so far have had little concern for all these aspects in the controlled market situation in which we operated in India (Dayal, 2004).

To sustain competitive edge in business, an organisation would have to develop their management systems, capabilities and approaches in many operational areas but most importantly; in generating the spontaneous will to cooperate among employees. Individuals at all levels have to use their own initiative to deal with situations and assume responsibility for results. We have seen repeatedly that people are extremely cooperative in one situation and the same people are totally indifferent to results in another situation. Cooperation is not entirely a function of an individual's predisposition but a response to situations where urge to achieve on their part is enhanced. There are some people who may lack the urge to improve for their own reasons or abnormalities. Many research studies have repeatedly shown that some persons who are seen to be shirkers at work are extremely devoted to many things that they do in another situation. Admittedly, some people are more efficient, work faster, have better comprehension than others, but the response to cooperate is independent of the capacity or skill to perform. And it is this characteristic that the situation at work has to generate. Research findings as well as recorded experience shows that people who feel involved in what they do, and are emotionally attached to the task in hand, give their best to the job. An important consideration for this state in the Indian situation is that an individual should feel that he is accepted in the work situation and belongs there. Acceptance means that the people with whom he interacts consider him to be one of them, and belonging means that he feels free to expose himself, if necessary, to share his anxieties and shortcomings, and seek help with the confidence that the people concerned would extend the help as do the family members back home. The social environment and the supervisory personnel should be able to evoke such feelings among individuals. In such an environment individuals are likely to be able to give their best. In situations where such feelings are not evoked, individuals are likely to do what they are asked to do and become what may be called clock watchers; they work for a living and seek relationships elsewhere.

The need for acceptance and belonging among individuals develop during the processes of growing up and remain imbedded in their psyche. The attitudes, sentiments and values so imbibed govern their responses to people and situations. If the individual encounters patterns of attitudes, values, relationships, etc. at work that are vastly different from those that are implanted in his unconscious mind in early years, the adjustment to that situation would require conscious effort. As the patterns of behaviour in his mind are spontaneous and unconscious, the nature of adjustment required on his part is not always understood by managers and he harbours a feeling of discomfort. In many cases he will carry out the task because he needs the work for survival but he would, in most cases, seek emotional adjustment elsewhere in other groups and situations. In this case, the probability is high that he separates work from his emotional, and essentially the creative self. Japan has developed work patterns which are in harmony with the wider society. In the industrial West the society has gradually absorbed the pattern of industrial work over the years. The dichotomy between work patterns in most organisations and the wider society in India is wide.

The Socialisation Process

Sociological and psychoanalytical studies show that basic attitudes, values, perceptions about people and things, develop in the process of growing up. Hence, we surveyed the studies of child-rearing practices in various communities in India and USA to derive from these the attitudes, values, etc. that individuals imbibe. These characteristics are shown in adult behaviour as well.

While there are some differences in child-rearing practices in some regions of the country, the essential characteristics in the Indian situation are common. Broadly these practices show caring and nurturing of children through physical contact, feeding, constant attendance on child's needs, etc. All this provides a sense of security and a feeling of belonging. This feeling is not conditional, *i.e.* if you do what I say or what I want you to do, you will receive attention in the family otherwise not. This kind of support and nurturing is ever present. Through many practices of the kind mentioned here, an individual develops a sense of strong attachment to the family. When the mother is busy, other members of the family treat children in the same way because in most joint families distinction between yours and mine is not visible. (Whiting, 1968; Spratt, 1968; Carstains, 1957; Dayal, 1977). The child's needs are attended to. He or she becomes a part of a group and learns from observation and relationships with others the right and the wrong ways of behaviour, values and attitudes etc. This is the group that provides the notion of social roles, role differentiation, social status, authority and different ways of reacting to people and things. This is the process of primary socialisation. Members of the extended family develop a bond and help individuals during illness, marriage of family members, and by providing financial support when required. This is the reason why membership of the community is so important for a family and for individuals.

Most individuals have their role models—invariably parents, uncles, brothers or teachers. A child observes that younger people extinguish their cigarette when an elder person enters the room. The child, thus learns that a person does not smoke in front of an elder. The girl child observes that women in the household react to situations differently, and a distinction is made between her and her brother in certain respects and slowly she understands her role in the family. Such attitudes do develop through abstract images formed in the mind and many of them retained in the unconscious mind. They do not develop through rational argument or even formal processes. The notions imbibed in the individual's mind guide responses in certain situations. Through this process, individuals in the family develop certain common responses to social situations. They also expect and anticipate certain responses from the elders, peers, people in authority and so on. If the responses are different, they rarely establish emotional links with such people. In the same way, individuals in certain communities have similar responses in certain ways. In adult life individuals respond to situations and people through these patterns that lie in their unconscious self. Certain patterns familiar to an individual are likely to create positive emotional responses, and unfamiliar patterns could lead to withdrawal. It is also likely that the individual could seek those individuals and groups in which the individuals respond in anticipated or familiar ways. For example, an individual in a company would seek out and become a member of a union if he feels more comfortable with the way they accept and deal with him than the company management. He might blindly follow people who share his background because they provide positive association with people who were good to him or cared for him. This is not a logical process but something that happens in the unconscious mind.

The description of socialisation here is highly simplified. It is intended to suggest the process of how attitudes, values, sentiments, etc. are acquired by individuals and carried by them in adult life.

The Predominant Indian Behavioural Characteristics

The studies of child-rearing practices, and a number of other studies, have brought out some common behavioural characteristics of Indian adults.

- Collective – strong bonds with family/ community
- Dependence upon others
- Tolerance and accommodation of people with different orientation
- Conflict – primarily psycho-social, less intra-psychic
- Conservative/traditional

- Accept authority specially from elders
- Passive/submissive
- Highly religious/spiritual

These characteristics contribute to acquiring emotional stability, and imbibing traditional attitudes and values. I believe that the values and attitudes that contribute most to the quality of life of individuals and contribute to their emotional self are the following:

- Collective – strong bonds with family/ community
- Tolerance and accommodation to people
- Authority from elders or respect for age
- Spirituality, having faith in something beyond oneself

If these attributes contribute to the emotional strength of people, they are also significant for quality of life of the community. This consideration is also necessary in the work place for building cooperative relationships and accepting responsibility for results in the job. The question is—how can such conditions be created at work which could induce emotional involvement of employees? Management system and practices should be able to develop these conditions to generate positive responses from employees. This has been done in Japan and some companies in India.

How have Leading Industrial Countries Achieved Harmony—the Case of Japan

In the developed industrial countries (mostly in the West), the transition from predominantly agricultural to industrial values developed over more than a hundred years. Over a period of time, and through generations, the values at work and in the community mutually influenced one another and evolved a set of shared values. The transition was natural without any plan on the part of the community and industry. However, traditional societies are called upon to adjust to the requirements of industry in a very short time; yet the harmony between the social environment of both is necessary.

American literature in management has influenced the ideas in teaching and practices in management. The practices prescribed in literature are largely based on the empirical research in organisations by academics and the experiences of many successful managers in United States and Europe. These ideas and practices which were seen as the right way to manage have been evolved and in some ways tested in the United States. In post-World War II, the success of Japanese business enterprises raised many questions in respect to absoluteness of the ideas that were found in the American literature. In a large measure, the Japanese had learnt some of the ideas in the United States but adapted them to their own social and cultural milieu–Basically, the need for adaptation related to the social and human processes that characterised the Japanese society. For example, they evolved consensus building, acceptance of authority, concerns about security and human bonds, work habits, etc. Japan brought these practices into management styles and practices from the wider society. The notions of loyalty to family and the group, in the wider society, were recreated in the work situation. Some of these developed into practices that became known as TQM, Kaisan and so on.

In sociological terms, two important notions are relevant for our immediate purpose in India: (i) there was harmony in the social system, attitudes, values in the wider society and the social organisation at work, (ii) the emotional and psychological aspects of individuals were mainly satisfied in terms of operating practices such as consultation, belonging to a social group, recognition, etc. The Japanese, or any other, management has to be concerned about efficiency, quality, cost, innovation, and all that the American management had developed through experience, practise and research. The Japanese, however, realised these goals through structures and processes that harmonised with their own societal norms and practices. This approach avoided a dichotomy between the right things at home and the same being not right at work. To a large extent Japan benefited by the fact that a few people who went to USA to study various practices returned and translated these ideas to fit in the prevailing culture in their own society. Further, Japan relied heavily on in-company training centers for education and training rather than the university system. Hence the teaching was primarily oriented to company requirements. The outside training establishments which grew in, large numbers also emphasised efficiency, the Japanese way of doing work, and hard-core practices. Management theory and practices began to be taught at the university level in more recent time.

In brief, the Japanese management practices relating to people are essentially based on the values, traditions and norms prevailing in the wider society. Individuals are easily able to interpret the meaning conveyed through the language, the network of relationships, and authority patterns. In this context, the management pay special attention to people and evolve practices that involve them in the core aspects of organisational activity.

Relevance of the Japanese Experiences for other Countries

The concerns for business are universal: efficiency, cost, quality, profitability, innovation, creative application to improve performance, and change. At the core of all these activities are people who perform to their optimum capacity by either coercion or willing cooperation. Coercion in human society invariably has counterforce in the short or the long-term. It also limits human capacity to innovate or create. The history of industrial work shows that willing cooperation is perhaps the only long-term measure that can provide the conditions for success. Research data and experience of successful organisations suggests that willingness to cooperate is a reaction and a response to the situation in which an individual is placed. The same person can be cooperative in one situation and, hostile in another. The same person can also be creative and totally rigid in two different situations. The same individual reacts to organisational practices differently and in this context of the culture, traditions, feelings, sentiments in a particular society are relevant for management. As discussed earlier, Japan was able to create a harmonious social environment in organisations which provided a base for achieving high performance standards. The increasing contact with the West, greater facility with english language, and prosperity in Japan are beginning to change the lifestyle of the younger generations, and with this change, the family and community relationships, attitudes, etc. will also change. If the business organisations fail to re-adjust their management practices consistent with changing realities, I suspect the social harmony, productivity and performance may suffer.

In the West, the process of social adaptation to industrial life was achieved over a long period of time starting with the Industrial Revolution. The focal point of change appears to be the demands that the most dominant institutions make on individuals. In money economy employment is necessary for survival. The attitudes and values prevailing in business organisations, and its values and way of life, is absorbed by employees. This process may take a generation or two. In Japan, the process was reversed. The organisation and management systems were adapted to the societal values, attitudes and sentiments. I believe in most developing countries the harmony at the work place, and therefore efficiency, individual initiative for quality and productivity, etc. would result from congruence between the societal and the organisational practices.

The Indian Management

Traditional societies, and most so called developing societies at that, have to encourage people in the organisation to achieve "a will to cooperate" in order to compete in global markets. This is necessary to be able to reduce costs, improve product quality, productivity, efficiency, and creativity at all levels of the organisation. Technological upgradation is necessary, but by its introduction as purely hardware, the organisation cannot achieve desired results without adequate preparation to effectively use the upgraded technology. Many organisations have heavily invested in technology without developing the system as a whole, including people, and failed to derive the advantages that technology is capable of giving.

In a developing country organisations have another responsibility. As in other countries, the dominant organisations which provide security and livelihood to people influence the attitudes and values that organisations instill in them. These, in turn, are transmitted through them to their families and the society as a whole. If the country should retain values which most leaders in India consider desirable such as strong family and community bonds, spiritualism, tolerance, respect for elders and the like, that provide foundation quality of life in India, these sentiments would have to be reflected in the social system of the organisation. Some years ago the British Prime Minister John Major expressed the need to re-acquire the old family values which, in the main, were lost in the years following the Industrial Revaluation. The US Presidents have also expressed similar concerns. I doubt that such sentiments could possibly be regained in these societies. If we believe that the kind of values mentioned here are important, for our countries to maintain quality of life, in India, they would have to be reflected in the management of organisations. Hence, two issues need special consideration of organisational management.

- Take a cue from the Japanese experience of developing management systems that harmonise with the wider culture and tradition, and

- Perpetuate the desired values and attitudes in our culture so that our society does not loose them in the same way the West has done.

The Implications for Management

If emotional involvement of employees is important, as I believe it is, there is apparent need for harmonising the patterns prevailing in the wider society and the work situation. This situation is likely to prevail if employees experienced at least two prime considerations:

- A feeling that the individual is a member of the work community and is accepted as such by his/her peers and superiors
- The norms of the work community are largely similar to what he/she has experienced in the back-home community which are familiar to him/her.

When the employee is fully integrated in the work community and the organisation, he is likely to experience a bond between the company and himself; and he is more likely to work for the well-being and growth of the company. He is likely to create value for the company by creative application of his skills. Some guidelines to develop a situation of mutual acceptance based on literature and experience are discussed below:

1. The employee should not be seen as an isolated individual but as a member of the family. The social

system of the company should see family and not the individual as a unit. Some of the ways in which companies have experienced this notion are:

(i) organising education/training/skill or literacy classes for the family

(ii) formally organising visits of family members to the factory to see how work is done

(iii) organising cooperatives of family members to engage in productive work

(iv) providing educational facilities for children

(v) organising social functions for employees and their families with top and senior management at periodic intervals.

These and some of the practices followed by companies, but there are possibly a great many other activities to bring families closer to the organisation.

2. As far as possible work should be organised in identifiable groups, and not individual assignments. Group work and shared responsibility among members helps in developing interacting relationships and a social group. Many examples of the arrangement are available in publications on the subject.

3. Supervision of work has to include personal relationships, besides work related issues. The

supervisors have to develop competence and skills in dealing with groups, problem-solving as against fault-finding attitude, interpersonal competence, and sensitivity towards human processes.

4. While administrative channels for decision-making are necessary to avoid chaos in the organisation, individuals should have access to anyone they feel necessary to approach to discuss their ideas or problems. Wilfred Brown refers to this arrangement as looped communication. CMC, prior to take over by the present management, followed this system. In the Indian Institute of Management at Lucknow we followed this system with great advantage. Many fresh ideas came from individuals down the line. IIM, Lucknow also developed the practice of an open house where anyone could ask questions, offer explanations and give suggestions. There are accounts of many organisations where this practice is followed with great effect.

5. Group working and urge to improve would be enhanced if the notion to compete with oneself *i.e.* to set goals to do better one's own performance, is promoted rather than competition. Research data shows that processes that lead to cooperation are different from those that generate differences among people and conflict. This notion is

consistent with the ethos of the Indian culture and tradition.

There are many organisations in India which have followed many of the ideas mentioned here. The most successful organisations, much before formal mnagement programmes were introduced in India, followed family-like patterns. One of the most successful and highly respected leaders in early 20th century, Lala Shri Ram of DCM Group, was seen by employees as a father figure. He visited every department on Holi festival and played symbolic Holi with workers. When the company was in financial trouble, he cut his own salary and others followed his example. When differences between the Mill management and workers could not be resolved, workers wanted Lala Shri Ram to be the arbitrator. Even as chairman and almost a builder of the business he led a very simple life and followed the open-door policy.

In Mafatlal Group, on festival occasions, employees came to show respect by touching the feet of the chairman. Many other organisations like TVS, T.I. Cycle Group and others also follow established traditions. I think we have to reflect seriously on the practices followed by top leaders in the country and derive how the culture of the company and the wider society can be harmonised.

References

Carstains, G M (1957). *The Twice-Born*, Hogarth Press, London.

Dayal, I et. al., (2007). *Family Managed, Multinationals and Public Sector Enterpises*, Ane Books India, New Delhi.

Dayal, I (2004). *Sustaining Growth in Organisation,* The ICFAI University Press, Hyderabad.

Dayal, I (1977). *Change in Work Organisation,* Concept, New Delhi.

Spratt, P (1968). *Hindu Culture and Personality,* Manakfala, Mumbai.

Whiting, B (1968). *Six Cultures-Studies of Child Rearing,* Wiley, New York.

8

University and Industry Link for Manpower Development

In India, there is repeated complaint about non-availability of qualified and talented people by academic, business and professional organisations. It is said that growth would suffer due to manpower shortages. At the same time, it is universally accepted that, intellectually, Indians are as good as any one from any other country. There is persuasive evidence to substantiate both these claims. Organisations are also concerned about the high turnover of good talent in spite of substantial increase in salaries and perks.

Concerns of this nature require both the industry and the educational system to jointly review the problem. Both have a role in resolving specific and general problems that concern client organisations.

Industries have to seriously question their assumptions about their own role in the migration of the manpower, and move away from the blame-game. They need to seriously look at why some organisations have a better record of retaining employees than others (Herzberg et. al., 1960; McClelland, 1961). In a developing country problem of shortages in respect to qualified manpower are to be expected especially when the nature of the business situation and consequent requirements of industrial organisations has become more demanding. Solutions that work in established industrial societies may not apply in our situation. They may have to work with educational institutions to devise specific programmes of training and education. This is being done by some organisations such as Pantaloon, ONGC, Gail, large IT businesses and others. Standard or mechanical approaches to deal with this problem are unlikely to apply to the local situation.

In the United States, and other countries in the West, the effort to upgrade the quality of education is made by the educational institutions themselves. This is so because the market will fail to support them if their standards are poorer than required by the market. Neither the government nor the Associations of business schools have any say in the matter. In India, the markets, as yet, have not developed discriminating capabilities to support or discourage poor quality of the educational programme. A few top companies have begun to do so, but their influence on internal systems at the institutional level are, as yet, weak. For example, the business hopes that by paying more money they will attract the talent. Another organisation whips the talent away by paying even more. If money and perks alone bind the individual to the organisation then this game will be played over and over again. The government keeps opening new institutions, or introduces new measures to increase the pool of available manpower without taking simultaneous action to improve the quality of education that is necessary to make more people employable. Teaching institutions load the faculty with more and more courses to teach without initiating measures to improve the quality of education. This action combined with the dysfunctional regulatory system, does little to change the situation. Each organisation works on its own without meaningful consultation with others. In essence, they work at cross purposes and fail to work towards shared goals. (Dayal, et. al., 2001)

Some Concerns

Three areas that have significantly contributed to the unemployablity of available manpower need attention. These are critical to solve the underlying infirmities that have greatly contributed to the present situation. These three areas have to do with:

- The Educational System
- The Approach of Business Organisations
- The Institutional Management

The problems of manpower shortages and quality are genuine and would need systematic action in all the three areas identified here. Piecemeal solutions like reservation of seats for students from underprivileged families or groups, geographical dispersal of institutions, etc. that we have attempted so far may have solved certain social problems but fail to address the issues. In fact, the question of opening doors for the deprived groups also needs a shared solution. The concerns of business that their competitive capability by indiscriminate measures, is as important as the governments' concern for creating opportunities for such groups. It is possible that by involving the concerned people alternatived measures, could have been found.

The Educational System

Institutions are made by teachers. The quality of education is directly related to the effectiveness of the teacher. Hence, the question is—what will encourage the teacher to improve himself? I have no personal experience with the school system but having spent close to 50 years in postgraduate teaching and directing management education, my comments refer mainly to that system. However, some things apply equally to all human beings. The critical factors are discussed below:

What will induce a person to 'think' and not do things in a mechanical way? There should be a sense of

'I have contributed to the achievement of our results'. In operational terms, a person has to have some say in how he can help achieve better results. He must have the opportunity to interact with others and explore new ideas. He must receive feedback that will help him to appraise himself and his own strengths and weaknesses. And the systems should be such that they encourage him to improve himself. While we may not be able to uniformly facilitate the development of all teachers at the same time, measures have to be put in place that can help individuals grow to their optimum capacity. This should really be the primary concern of a regulatory body at the level of the educational system as a whole and also of the Institutional Management. Instead, our regulatory bodies at both these levels seem to be more concerned about regulation (standardisation) and control. They control the curriculum, the books to be used, the examination system, and the behaviour of the teacher. Any deviation from the prescriptive requirements is discouraged by both the regulatory system, and the institution concerned. In university level courses in functional areas, teachers teach and most students learn to pass examinations by memorising the text. There are a handful of students who take their studies seriously, and not merely to pass examinations as prescribed by the programme. The purpose of a professional programme such as management, law, medicine, etc., is to enable students to internalise knowledge and instinctively use it to understand and resolve business, organisational, societal and personal problems. In fact, there are a large number of privately funded institutions which have an unwritten policy not to fail a student. The system demands no originality, or any creative output, either from the teacher or the student.

Some readers would regard these remarks as extreme. I would only urge them to look at the data provided by many surveys carried out by several committees set up by the government and the regulatory bodies (Dayal et. al., 2001). The HRD ministry is occupying itself with increasing numbers of seats in institutions, which in turn, will continue to produce, by and large unemployable people and at best serve as employment agencies, and not knowledge creating institutions. The regulatory agency for technical education–AICTE–seems hardly concerned with the problem of building requisite quality of manpower. Solutions are available in a plethora of reports on the subject, but action can only be taken by people who are willing to appreciate the problems and are interested in resolving these.

The Approach of Business Organisations

Around 50 years ago when I served in an executive position, we forecast our manpower requirements at all levels of the operating and managerial positions and recruited people as trainees and gave them the best possible training to suit our requirements. The training consisted of both classroom sessions and on-the-job training. The programme was carefully monitored and reviewed by higher management at appropriate intervals. I am aware of many organisations that did similar exercises to meet their manpower requirements. Admittedly, because of rapid economic growth, now the numbers of people are many more, but the problem remains the same. In view of the educational system remains frozen in the past, business organisations must collaborate with willing educational institutions to improve the quality of their inputs. They can use a select number of institutions to meet the training needs of their personnel. Instead, the business assumes that, as in the West, they should be able to meet their manpower requirement from the open market, which, sadly, they are not able to.

The business organisations, as other institutions, have to view the problem in a historical perspective. We have to recognise that an overwhelming majority of families do not, or are not able to, send their children to school. This figure of children going to school is likely to be much smaller than that of literacy in the country. Hence the pool of children finishing school is rather small. In a large number of cases the parents are illiterate. Whatever the children learn, they do so in school. Apart from a few urban schools, the emphasis is primarily on subject teaching, not on developing a student as a person.

It is hard to believe that knowledgeable and intelligent persons in the ministry are not aware of the reality. It is apparent that without basic changes, the educational system is unlikely to serve the need for developing individuals who can take objective decisions. The oft repeated notion of private-public collaboration has not served its purpose because a majority of privately financed and managed institutions have been dwarfed by the regulatory control in education and the compelling need of the promoters to control the system. As in the post World War II period in the United States, people with influence have to exert pressure on the government to strive towards a political consensus to undertake needed reforms. Personally I doubt if the recommendations of the Knowledge Commission in respect to educational reforms will go far enough to remove the infirmities of the educational system.

As business grows and becomes a dominant economic entity, replacing the government's position in this regard, and also as a significant provider of livelihood, it will influence through its own employees, and also in a direct way through media and other means, the way of life of families and people in society at large. The values and attitudes that prevail in the workplace will also transmit to society. This has happened in all countries in the West and the beginning of this phenomenon is noticeable in parts of urban India. If business leaders recognise the socio-psychological processes that influence society, they would also be concerned about the kind of society in which their children, and they themselves, would like to live. Besides the vision and mission of their businesses, they would have equal concern for societal values and attitudes. They would have to promote, within the organisation, the attitudes and values they believe make people in the society live a healthy life. Business education too would have to be concerned about a manager's role in terms of developing a socially strong human organisation and an individual's role as a citizen. Business education, as it did in the past, should provide what Oxford and Cambridge did in the UK, *i.e.* liberal education. The programme should conceive a citizen-manager role apart from teaching the core commercial areas.

There is a tendency among a large number of organisations (and institutions) to copy the practices that are associated with success in the West. The socio-psychological environment in the two situations, the West and the Indian, is different. The practices that we follow have been based on the foundations of the Indian society. One chief executive of a large multinational company summarised the essence of our discussion by saying that to succeed in India in real sense a chief executive should understand the sociology of Indian people.

In USA, the business and other organisations rely heavily on the university system. In India, a few top and senior personnel are associated with our educational system as individuals, but rarely as an organisation. They have to learn to reject poor quality of education and the graduates that such institutions produce. There is mutual gain in such association. Large business houses who are setting up their own institutions hardly serve any purpose because their quality of output is no different from that of other existing institutions. Exceptions can be counted on one's fingertips.

There is yet another concern that is often expressed in conversation and in reports. Employees leave jobs for small financial gains. More than sixty years of authentic research in social sciences has clearly demonstrated that beyond a certain level of income and perks, it is the satisfaction in performing the job, work autonomy, and achievement as perceived by the individual concerned that is more important in order to involve him in what he does, (Herzberg, 1960). Without fulfillment the latter condition, individuals will continue to drift. They will not settle down to a job, or even be proud of themselves. It is this aspect that would contribute to an acceptable level of stability in an organisation. People need to respect themselves to be happy with what they do.

A business organisation, in the present economic environment, has a decisive influence on society. To treat it merely as a wealth generating institution is denying the reality of the social situation.

Institutional Management

Barring a few institutions, subjects are taught in the way they teach subject-based courses in a college. The management in most institutions accept the prescribed requirements of the regulatory bodies. Institutions provide no funds and little encouragement to undertake research, or upgrade their knowledge base; these matters are routinely brought up in review committees on management education. There is little pressure either from business organisations or regulatory bodies to improve quality of inputs. The management's primary concern is to somehow find jobs for all students, as failure in this will adversely affect applications for admission, and in turn, their financial position. The quality of education in many institutions that follow this model will undergo drastic change only if business organisations refuse to accept their standards of education. This hasn't happened because most institutions provide a ready list of somewhat above average students which saves organisations their cost of recruitment. Companies that require higher standard visit only those institutions which are rated highly by the rating agencies. The existing procedures to rate the suitability or standard of education employed by regulatory bodies is unlikely to induce change in standards of educational proramme. As things stand, individuals shine on their own strength and most of us believe that they would do so even if they never came to a business school, except a fairly small number who are deeply concerned with the programme of study.

The consequence of the prevailing approaches in a very large number of institutional management and that of the regulatory bodies is that no research and innovation at the institution level would happen. And lack of these would fail to develop thinking on the part of teachers or students. In spite of long association with a number of institutions and membership of governing boards of several, I have yet to come across effective governance in respect to academic performance. A large number of governing bodies are concerned about evolving "revenue models" more than upgrading educational standards. To a large extent, these concerns reflect on the composition of the boards and the sponsor-owner influence in many privately funded institutions.

In brief, educationists have not succeeded in changing the basic approaches to reform the system. Some have withdrawn from the exercise and some have left the country. The enormous price that the nation has paid, and continues to pay, is gross waste of talent in the country. Perhaps a combined efforts of business leaders, who have clout based on their economic performance and academics could compel the people concerned with national polices to seriously review the system. Personally, I hope this would happen.

References

Dayal, I et.al., (2001). *Report on Future Directions for Management Education*, Government of India, New Delhi.

Herzberg, F; Mausner, B and Snydermaumm (1960). *The Motivation to Work*, Wiley, New York.

McClellant, D C (1961). *Achieving Society,* The Free Press, New York.

Authors' Index